PRACTICAL PARENTING GUIDE

PARENT TIPS

BY RON & LORI TERMALE

VISIT OUR FB AND INSTAGRAM PAGE FOR MORE INSIGHT AND FUN TIPS **@PARENTTIPSBOOK**

Copyright © 2024 by Ron and Lori Termale

ISBN: 9798338967010

All rights reserved.

No portion of this book may be reproduced in any form without written permission from the publisher or author, except as permitted by U.S. copyright law.

Book design and illustrations by Josmary Rivera
Josyrivera63@gmail.com

Book cover by Carissa Termale
SolCoffeeCart@gmail.com

We dedicate this book to our three children Michael, Daniel and Carissa, and thank them for filling our lives with so much joy.

We also honor our parents, Giovanni Termale, who is in heaven, and Eva Termale, now 93 years of age. Special thanks to Ron and Cheryl Paliotta for taking on the role of godly parents to Lori. There is so much we have learned from your example, and we love you very much.

Much appreciation to our Pastors Stephen and Nancy Boyce, and close friends Michael and Pamela Corcoran, and Michael and Barb Servello for walking alongside us in the journey called life. You have been a blessing to our family.

Table of Contents

Acknowledgements   i

Introduction   iii
- How to use this book

Parent Tips

1. The buck stops with you   01

2. Invest in yourself   07

3. Get rid of your baggage   13

4. No such thing as a bad child   21

5. Authority brings security   29

6. Priorities, persistence, protection   37

7. The importance of a talk   45

Table of Contents

8. Decision making — 53

9. Engineering friendships — 61

10. Making memories — 71

11. Sexuality: when and how? — 77

12. Strong-willed children — 83

13. Daycare and education — 91

14. Yes, no, maybe — 101

15. Who runs your house — 107

16. Big ears — 115

17. Happiness is not the goal — 121

Table of Contents

18. Reasoning with a child   129

19. Different strokes for different folks   137

20. Manners matter   145

21. A strong will can be a future benefit   151

22. Freedom to choose   159

23. What discipline is not   165

24. Your child has a destiny   173

25. Bring on the laughter   183

26. Pray, pray, pray   189

Acknowledgements

Both Lori and I have had the privilege of learning from people that have gone through great challenges. My immigrant parents survived World War II living under Nazi rule and experienced great hunger, loss and of course fear.

My mom Eva watched her parents and a young brother killed by the Nazis. As an orphan child along with her younger sister Iole, and brother Claudio, she had to endure living without food on the war-torn streets of Italy. After the war she also experienced harsh treatment in an orphanage.

Even though life was not easy, my mother and father never held onto regrets and bitterness. They worked hard and showed us through tragedy and with very little, there can always be love at home. I must add, my sister Patricia Corcoran, who also showed Lori and I how a single mom can overcome great challenges. She raised two successful children, Christopher and Sarah, both nurses.

My wife Lori experienced great challenges as well. Her mom passed away when she was only two years of age, and her dad when she was eleven. Lori was also in a terrible car accident when she was eight years of age, with her brother dying as a result.

When Lori was five, she was taken into the home of her older sister Cheryl and brother-in-law Ron. She was surrounded by faith, love and care and raised with her two nieces who she sees as sisters, Cherie Adams and Cathy Paliotta. Lori's experiences helped to mold her into one of the greatest moms I know. My children and so many others can testify to this fact.

Parenting is not easy; it takes a village. Over the years, we have sought advice from many and have watched how parents raise godly and successful children. We thank God for friends, family, a great church and wise pastors. This book is not only from our learning and experience, but it contains wisdom from all those that have been part of our lives and the resources we acknowledge in its pages.

We pray you are encouraged and equipped by this book of "Parent Tips".

"For I can do everything through Christ, who gives me strength."
Philippians 4:13 NLT

Introduction

As parents of three grown children and six grandchildren (to date), we have learned good parenting skills are not something you are born with, but learned.

Decades of pastoring and operating a daycare have provided us with great insight into family dynamics and parenting. But nothing beats hands-on practice and experience. Even education does not match on-the-job training.

People have their own definition of successful parenting and children. Some people see success as raising well-educated children that become financially affluent as adults. Their measuring rod is how much money their children make or the job title they may hold. Others measure success by comparing their children with the achievements of other children and the standards of this world.

We will define successful parenting as providing a child with the greatest opportunity to fulfill the will of God for their lives.
A successful parent helps to build a whole person who makes a difference in the lives of others. They live their lives with a sense of purpose, fulfillment, happiness, and faith in God.

Parenting is a collaboration of many factors, but there are certain keys or "Parent Tips" that can guide you in raising healthy, happy, and successful children. We hope to provide you with some "Parent Tips" that will make a difference in your life as a parent, as well as in the lives of your children.

My wife and I are so thankful for all the help we received in raising our children. They are all secure in their identity, strong in their faith and convictions, hard working, successful in their decision-making, giving, loving and kind to their fellow man.

When we look back at what shaped our children we give credit to prayer, teachings in scripture, the guidance of godly mentors, supportive friends and family, and the application of key principles.

We also thank God for a local church filled with dynamic children and youth ministries. The church provided an opportunity for our children to develop healthy godly relationships and to enjoy life with peers of like faith and values.

"Parent Tips" will provide you with the knowledge and wisdom we have gained over the years. We are sure "Parent Tips" will be of great benefit to you.

How to use this book:

This book is a manual for parenting that should be read slowly and completely, and used throughout your parenting years. It can also be used as a daily devotional, a small group resource and for sharing with parents.

We highly recommend this book for small group meetings, discussion and learning. Use it to gather parents together for encouragement, support and to develop new friends.

(Parent Tip #1)

THE BUCK STOPS WITH YOU

"Direct your children onto the right path, and when they are older, they will not leave it." Proverbs 22:6 NLT

"Listen, my son, to your father's instruction and do not forsake your mother's teaching. They are a garland to grace your head and a chain to adorn your neck." Proverbs 1:8-9 NIV

➤ **One of the most important tips for parenting is knowing it is a parent's responsibility to instruct and raise their child(ren). No one else!**

It is not the responsibility of a daycare, school, relatives, friends, babysitters, or anyone or anything else for a child's life, their moral compass, their spiritual, emotional and cognitive development. There are many influences impacting children, but it is a parent's job to orchestrate who and what will influence their child. It is a parent's responsibility to mold, shape, protect, provide for and care for their child's well-being.

➤ **There is no such thing as being an overprotective parent.**

You can never be an overprotective parent if your decisions are formed by love, wisdom, prayer, Biblical principles, and are for the best interest of your child. We are not to live in fear or parent in fear, but we are to parent with wisdom and discernment. A parent's first duty is to protect their child and to create a safe and nurturing environment. **Convenience cannot supersede what is best for your child.** Who you leave your child with and where you leave your child must be covered by thought, prayer, wisdom and references.

A Story

We had a rule in our home, one of many. There is no sleeping over someone else's house if we do not know the parent or parents well. It doesn't matter if the parents attend the same church with us, live in the same neighborhood, or if their children are over our home all the time. Another rule was, it is ok for any of our children's friends to stay overnight at our home.

Well, we were sometimes labeled as being overprotective and unfair. We heard this from our children and their friends, as well as their friends' parents. We would be asked why can my child stay at your home, but yours cannot stay at our home? Seems hypocritical right? Not at all. Every parent must do what they feel is right for their own children. We were responsible for the raising of our children, not the children of others.

Unless we were confident that our children would not be exposed to anything that would be harmful to their physical, emotional, psychological, and spiritual well-being, the answer to their requests for overnight stays would be "No". Why? Because dad and mom love you so much that we have rules to protect you.

As a parent you have to be willing to be unpopular. God has a way of supporting you as a parent when you are doing what is right in His eyes and for your kids.

Interesting

Written By Michael Greger M.D. FACLM on June 17, 2014
When researchers offered kids broccoli or a chocolate bar, which do you think they picked? Four out of five picked the chocolate (though how proud are the parents of the one in five kids that chose the broccoli?!). But what if we put an Elmo sticker on the broccoli? When an Elmo sticker was placed on the broccoli, it was half and half. Fifty percent chose broccoli.

BOTTOM LINE

- It's a parent's responsibility, no one else, to raise their children.
- There is no such thing as being an overprotective parent.
- Convenience cannot supersede what is best for your child.

Small Group Discussion Questions

What really spoke to you in this "Parent Tip"?

What would you change in your parenting because of this "Parent Tip"?

Do you have any suggestions regarding this "Parent Tip" topic?

Today's Prayer

LORD, I pray you bless and prosper me as a parent. Thank you for giving me the desire to learn and to practice the keys to raising healthy, happy and prosperous children. In Jesus' Name, I pray. Amen!

"The Lord bless you and keep you; the Lord make his face shine on you and be gracious to you; the Lord turn his face toward you and give you peace." Numbers 6:24-26 NIV

Personal Reflection

Parent Tip #2

INVEST IN YOURSELF

"Beloved, I pray that all may go well with you and that you may be in good health, as it goes well with your soul."
3 John 1:2 ESV

▶ **You must get and stay healthy.**

Your kids need the best of you. Healthy children come from healthy parents. This means you need to take time for yourself, and if married, invest in your marriage. You need to evaluate your life and what you are doing to stay healthy, body, soul and spirit.

You should not feel guilty about finding time for yourself. Obviously as a parent you have less time than those who do not have children, but you still have time to think through your life and to determine what you need to do to **relax, refresh and rejuvenate.**

Some people find exercising as their way to reduce stress, others read, and yet others just need some quiet time alone. Whatever you need to do to be a better you, do it! People who invest in themselves spiritually, emotionally and physically have greater energy for parenting. **Do not feel guilty about caring for yourself.**

▶ **A great way to stay spiritually and emotionally healthy is being active in a local church community.**

A good church provides spiritual and emotional support for you and your children. Church activities, small groups and ministry involvement, all create opportunities for friendships to develop with like-minded parents. Many single parents and young married families in our church support each other in their parenting roles.

This helps them to find free time to maintain their physical, spiritual and emotional health. What a great benefit to parents! Church is also a great place to find trustworthy sitters for your children.

"For where two or three are gathered in my name, there am I among them." Matthew 18:20

A Story

My wife and I have always lived busy lives. When we started having children I was a Bank Vice President, my wife ran a home daycare business. We were also very involved in our local church. Our home was always filled with people and ministry, and somehow we were able to properly care for our children, get enough rest, and be happy as a married couple.

Establishing routine and structure for our children brought great benefit to our parenting, marriage and family dynamics. We encourage setting routines for children for their benefit as well as yours. One of those routines is having a set bedtime. Children need rest, structure and routine. Generally, at 7:00PM we began the process of bedtime and by 8PM lights were out. We did make exceptions for church night, which our children loved, and other special occasions. Having a set routine for children creates time for parents to relax, refresh and rejuvenate.

Daycare parents would sometimes complain to my wife about their children being unruly while being compliant for my wife.

A Story (continued)

The reason for this was lack of structure and routine at home. My wife had a consistent daily routine for her daycare children. She maintained order. Children feel secure when they experience a consistent routine, boundaries and structure.

Interesting

Taken from "Zero to Thrive" - University of Michigan
https://zerotothrive.org/routines-for-kids/

Why routines matter

Research shows that routines support healthy social emotional development in early childhood. In particular, children with regular routines at home have self-regulation skills, the building blocks of good mental health. When children learn to regulate feelings and behaviors, it means they are able to identify their feelings and have skills to manage those feelings so that they don't feel overwhelmed. Young children who learn to do this well are better able to adapt to everyday challenges, stressors, and new expectations. Children do not learn to do this all at once. Just as when a child is learning other important skills, like reading and writing, self-regulation is a set of skills that build over time. Every stage includes age-appropriate milestones and important things parents can do to coach children from one stage into the next.

BOTTOM LINE
- Find time for yourself to stay spiritually, emotionally and physically healthy.
- A church community is extremely beneficial to the well being of parents and children.
- Children need structure and routine, and parents need time to relax, refresh, and rejuvenate.

Small Group Discussion Questions

What really spoke to you in this "Parent Tip"?

What would you change in your parenting because of this "Parent Tip"?

Do you have any suggestions regarding this "Parent Tip" topic?

Today's Prayer

LORD, I pray you give me the ability to structure my days and establish routines that are beneficial to my children and me, spiritually, emotionally and physically. Give me a positive mindset and a can do attitude. In Jesus' Name, I pray. Amen!

"I can do all this through him who gives me strength."
Philippians 4:13 NIV

Personal Reflection

(Parent Tip #3)

GET RID OF YOUR BAGGAGE

"For in the same way you judge others, you will be judged, and with the measure you use, it will be measured to you."
Matthew 7:2 NIV

➤ Do not carry baggage into parenting.

As adults, we can all look back and critique a parent's right decisions, wrong decisions, good parenting and bad parenting. We know their flaws, imperfections, behavior patterns, as well as their strengths, weaknesses, and the benefits and hurts they brought into our lives. We have good memories and bad memories, hopefully, more positive than negative.

Some people have great regrets when it comes to the experiences they have had with their parents and others that have impacted their lives. At times, thoughts and memories flood their minds, mostly bad. Even in adulthood some still psychologically and emotionally relive the behavior of those who were supposed to care and encourage them, protect and provide for them and create a secure upbringing. Your memories and emotions may be getting stirred right now as you read this paragraph, thus, the influence of a parent and others involved in the lives of children. But now it's your turn! You can learn from the past mistakes of others and become a better parent.

➤ To be a healthy person and parent you must forgive.

Not forgiving, not letting go of past hurts, keeps you locked up in a cage of bitterness. It is critical to get set free from the negativity and hurts of the past. We all have deep emotions, both good and bad, that can greatly influence our adulthood and parenting.

We must keep the good and rid ourselves of hurts and negativity. We do not want to hold on to anything that will hurt our children as well.

You must let go of resentment towards anyone who has harmed you emotionally, psychologically and physically. Otherwise, you will end up parenting out of a polluted well, that will hurt the very ones you love. If unforgiveness is not dealt with, a seed of bitterness will be passed down to the next generation, your children. *Hurt people hurt people!*

➤ **You can only give what you have.**

Receiving forgiveness from God by the acceptance of Jesus Christ into one's life provides a reservoir of forgiveness by which to forgive others. When you experience and receive forgiveness you are able to give others what you yourself have received.

Salvation through Jesus Christ and receiving the Holy Spirit give you the power to release others who have hurt you. Jesus taught us to pray and ask God for forgiveness. In the LORD's Prayer, Jesus stipulates forgiveness is received as we forgive others. When we do not forgive others we hold back our own forgiveness. To be a good parent you must forgive and learn to live a life of grace and mercy.

"...and forgive us our sins, just as we have forgiven those who have sinned against us." Matthew 6:12

A Story

Growing up in an immigrant family, with lots of people in our home, there were many influences in my childhood. In addition to my parents, there were grandparents and two uncles living in a small apartment along with my sister and me. I remember receiving corrections from all different people. I am sure I needed some of it, but sometimes the smallest and most vulnerable receive the brunt of others' frustration, anger, and hostility.

Both my parents grew up in Italy during the Nazi occupation. My dad as a young boy was used for slave labor by German troops and my mom's parents and little brother were murdered in cold blood by the Nazi's. My mom's mother, my grandmother and her child, Umberto, were machine gunned down while waiting in a bread line. Her husband, my grandfather, died from a hand grenade being thrown into the crowd as he lamented over his wife's body.

My dad and his family became refugees during World War II. It was a very hard life. My mom at age 11 and her two younger siblings were placed in an orphanage until she was 18 years old. Both my dad and mom did not receive the love and attention needed as children, and thus, they could only give what they had received.

There was not much affirmation in our home except from my grandmother who became a second mother to me.

A Story (continued)

Both of my parents worked all day to achieve the American dream and to make a better life for their children. My dad worked two jobs and did not get home until 10PM on most nights. There was a longing inside of me for my parents' time, attention and input. I did not realize until later in life how this affected my thought patterns.

I had hidden bitterness towards my dad because he was not able to give me what I expected of him as a father, especially time and affection. I later learned that his dad, my grandfather, often said in Italian, "you don't kiss a child unless he or she is sleeping." Maybe he thought affirming children would make them weak. Not sure, but my father carried on this philosophy towards his children. You can only give what you have!

If I had not dealt with unforgiveness I would have become an unhealthy parent. **To be a good parent you must be a whole parent.** This cannot be stated enough! You as a parent must evaluate your personal strengths and weaknesses, and work on your weaknesses so they do not overtake your parenting.

Happy to say, when I turned 40 years old and was heading off on a missionary trip to Thailand, my dad came up to me and said the words I had been longing to hear from him, "I love you." It's never too late to make things right with your children.

Interesting

Below Taken from HuffPost.com - Dr. Randy Kamen, Contributor/Huffington Post | Updated December 26, 2012

Forgiveness means giving up the suffering of the past and being willing to forge ahead with far greater potential for inner freedom. Anne Lamott famously declared, "Forgiveness is giving up all hope of having had a different past." Besides the reward of letting go of a painful past, there are powerful health benefits that go hand-in-hand with the practice of forgiveness. In the physical domain, forgiveness is associated with lower heart rate and blood pressure as well as overall stress relief. It is also associated with improving physical symptoms, reducing fatigue in some patient populations, and improving sleep quality. In the psychological domain, forgiveness has been shown to diminish the experience of stress and inner conflict while simultaneously restoring positive thoughts, feelings, and behaviors.

BOTTOM LINE

- The hurts of the past will be passed onto your children if you do not get free from them.
- Forgiveness is necessary to become a whole and healthy person/parent.
- You can learn from your parent's weaknesses as well as their strengths.

Small Group Discussion Questions

What really spoke to you in this "Parent Tip"?

What would you change in your parenting because of this "Parent Tip"?

Do you have any suggestions regarding this "Parent Tip" topic?

Today's Prayer

LORD, help me to become whole as a person and parent. I forgive those who have hurt me and ask for forgiveness for anything I have done or said to my child(ren) out of bitterness and anger. Thank you God for your grace and mercy. Amen!

"Let love and faithfulness never leave you; bind them around your neck, write them on the tablet of your heart. Then you will win favor and a good name in the sight of God and man." Proverbs 3:3-4 NIV

Personal Reflection

Parent Tip #4

NO SUCH THING AS A BAD CHILD

"Children are a gift from the Lord; they are a reward from him." Psalm 127:3 NLT

Every child is a gift from God and a unique person from birth.
Every child is born with his or her own characteristics, personality, and tendencies. There are some traits passed down from generations past, but still every human being is created with their own spirit, will, gifts and talents which can be shaped.

In 1917, after working with Omaha's homeless men for years, Father Edward J. Flanagan opened Father Flanagan's Boys Home, which later became Boys Town. He championed the causes of children across the country. A movie about his life was played by a famous actor Mickey Rooney. One of the greatest quotes by Father Flanagan in the movie was "there is no such thing as a bad boy."

Can such a complex and wonderful creation, a human being, be molded into someone with a healthy identity, and positive behavior patterns? Can a child be developed by his or her parents into a successful and godly adult, or is everything predetermined by DNA and generational iniquities? The answer is yes; you certainly can raise children who will make you proud to be a parent. Children who are formed by godly parenting and mentoring become spiritually and emotionally healthy adults.

➤ There is no such thing as a bad child.

There used to be a TV program called **Nanny 911**. This documentary followed the lives of parents who were dealing with out-of-control children. The super nanny was called into a parent's home on a 911 emergency basis.

The parents could no longer deal with their child's or children's behavior patterns. As you begin to watch the program, your initial reaction is empathy towards the parents. It appears the parents were dealt a bad hand. You begin to think the child was born with serious issues of rebellion, anger and disobedience.

As the Nanny 911 program moves along, you come to realize the problem is not the child, but insufficient and or terrible parenting skills. Nanny 911 begins to adjust the child's behavior by changing the parent's behavior. The parents are to be taught the error of their ways, and learn the effective ways to parent a child. Little at a time the dynamics of the family begin to change and improve. What appears to be a hopeless situation becomes a model of a functional home with love, positivity, and correct parent-to-child relationships and vice versa.

Every Parent Tip will provide you with insight to help you reap positive results in the parenting of your child(ren).

➤ **You are not born a good parent; good parents are developed by learning, practice, work, and consistency.**

You may be asking, is it too late for me? You may be thinking my child is too old and is already displaying characteristics and behavior patterns detrimental to their well-being and success.

It is never too late to influence a child. You can be a good parent! Whether single or married you can raise children who will become successful adults.

There is always a path forward. and it is by obtaining knowledge and gaining wisdom.

"Get wisdom, get understanding; do not forget my words or turn away from them." Proverbs 4:5

- **Your sons and daughters do not need perfection, they need genuine love.**

Your child needs to see you giving your best and improving in how you communicate with them, spend time with them, invest in them, pray with them and ask for God to be involved in their lives. They need to see you working hard at being the best mom or dad you can be.

Do not let the guilt of past mistakes stop you from changing the future. Even your weaknesses and mistakes can be used to teach your children the importance of learning from them, improving and ultimately changing your behavior as a parent.

- **Your words have power! Your words will either build up or destroy.**

"And a voice from heaven said, "This is my Son, whom I love; with him I am well pleased." Matthew 3:17

A child's spirit is very sensitive to a parent's communication with them and in the home. You can easily bruise a child's spirit by what you say. and how you act and react with them.

A child needs to see your love as well as hear your love for them. The words, "I love you" should not be a rare communication. Remember your words have power!!

Children need to know you are proud of them and value them as individuals. Boys need to be admired and girls need to be cherished. Celebrate your child's accomplishments and comfort them in times when they feel defeated. **You are helping to form their identity.**

Decree over every child who God sees them as and who you want them to be, i.e. "You are a good boy, a good girl." "You are a leader and not a follower." "God has great plans for your life." "We are so proud of you.", etc. Pray over your child while they are awake and while they are asleep. Declare over them the hopes and aspirations God has for their lives. Your words, His Words, are like seeds planted in a field, they will germinate and produce the harvest planted.

➤ **Even if you do not feel qualified you are ordained by God with the authority to train and lead your children.**

You as a parent are specially chosen to receive and care for your gift from heaven. God sees your child as His special creation and He has entrusted him or her into your care.

It's OK to feel as though you may be failing at times. Most parents feel this way. Just assess where you are in your present parenting skills and work on improving them. **You can do it!**

Lori's Story

You learn a lot about children and parents when you operate a daycare. I ran a daycare in my home for 12 years. One of my policies was to tell parents there was a two week trial period to determine if my daycare was a good match for their child and me. This policy was not so much a test for the child, but more so a test for the parents. Will the parent be responsible in bringing and picking up their child on a timely basis? Were they willing to leave their children in a Christ centered daycare? Were their actions as adults safe for the children in my daycare and me, etc.?

There was one child in my daycare that tended to change personalities upon being picked up by the parents. The child would become greatly agitated and would begin screaming when one of the parents arrived at my home at the end of the day.

The parent would ask me, "How do you deal with this all day long?" It was shocking to hear this child was a terror at home. Under my care, the child was well-behaved.

I had the opportunity to spend time at the home of this child's parents. I realized the child was starving for attention. Both parents worked long hours and there was no order and structure in the household. The child's bad behavior was the result of a need for attention, peace and boundaries in the home. There is no such thing as a bad child, just parents needing to be trained.

BOTTOM LINE

- There is no such thing as a bad child, every child is a gift from God.
- You are not born a good parent, good parents are developed.
- Your words and actions are molding your child's identity.
- You are ordained by God with the authority to be a good parent.

Small Group Discussion Questions

What really spoke to you in this "Parent Tip"?

What would you change in your parenting because of this "Parent Tip"?

Do you have any suggestions regarding this "Parent Tip" topic?

Today's Prayer

LORD, guide me in your ways to be a better parent and to learn from my mistakes. Help me to use my words to build up my child(ren), to speak life into them, and to pray blessing over them daily. In Jesus' Name, Amen!

"Thy word is a lamp unto my feet, and a light unto my path."
Psalm 119:105

Personal Reflection

_____

_____

_____

_____

_____

_____

_____

_____

Parent Tip #5

AUTHORITY BRINGS SECURITY

"Everyone must submit to governing authorities. For all authority comes from God, and those in positions of authority have been placed there by God."
Romans 13:1

"Children, obey your parents in everything, for this pleases the Lord." Colossians 3:20 NIV

There is much confusion and difference of opinion regarding parenting, even among so-called experts. Some believe children should be treated as equals and it is not necessary to exercise authority over them. Their philosophy is children should have the right to self rule and you can reason with them at any age. They also see permissiveness as love and Biblical discipline as child abuse. This is contrary to the teachings of the Bible. The Bible teaches God gives you as a parent authority over your children.

Have you ever been embarrassed or felt sorry for the parent who had lost complete control over their child: Screaming, kicking, spitting, biting, demanding and head spinning in public with no fear of consequence? The response of the parent will show you who has the authority, the child or the parent.

▶ **The Bible teaches a parent must exercise authority and discipline in order to raise secure and successful children.**

The Bible teaches we are to raise children who are obedient, have faith in God and are not foolish. This will bring joy to you as a parent and not a painful burden. There will be more on discipline in upcoming "Parent Tips".

A child must obey his or her parents. This requires the exercise of a parent's role as the authority figure in the home, one who leads his or her children.

Yes and no, must mean exactly that. Parental authority in a family brings security to a child and order to the family structure. Every organization has a senior authority figure. In the home it is the parent. *The buck must stop with you!*

With authority comes great responsibility. You must respect, deeply love, have patience and gently instruct your children. Remember there is an authority greater than your authority and that is GOD! You will be accountable to Him as to how you care for the gift He has given you, your children.

➤ **If you as a parent do not require obedience, you will feed rebellion and insecurity.**

This character trait will follow your children into teen years and even adulthood, and thus causing you as a parent, and your children, much pain.

Requiring obedience is a lifesaver. It is what provides guardrails in a dangerous world. It is what shows your children you mean what you say and you say what you mean. It is what shows them they are worth your time, effort and instruction. Do not doubt the authority God has given you as a parent! Be convinced you have what your children need; knowledge, wisdom, experience and the capacity to protect and guide them.

Your kids are looking to be led. If you do not take the lead, they will look for someone who will lead them and will receive your lack of parenting as rejection.

I know it is difficult for some people to be bold, strong and unswerving in requiring obedience from their children. But do not be deceived into thinking because you do not have an authoritarian personality, your children will not listen to you.

Leading as a parent takes consistency, untiring commitment, and discipline. You can do it! Just think what would come of a child if a parent does not command and demand their children to not touch fire, to not cross a street without looking for oncoming traffic, or to not take a stranger's hand, etc. What would come of a child if they grow up believing there are no boundaries and consequences to their actions?

> **One of the most important commandments of the Bible is for children to honor and obey their parents.**

A parent has the final authority in the family. A child's obedience to a parent is their protection for living a long and happy life.

"Children, obey your parents in the Lord, for this is right. "Honor your father and mother"—which is the first commandment with a promise—so that it may go well with you and that you may enjoy long life on the earth." Ephesians 6:2-3

We live in a world filled with lawlessness and disrespect towards authority, including parents. Boundaries that have existed for generations are being torn down and redefined by culture. You must never abandon the Biblical pattern for raising children. You must expect your children to obey you and follow your lead.

God has given you His most precious gift and creation. You cannot leave the care of this gift to happenstance, guess work, and ever changing human philosophies. If there are no absolutes to parenting then there is nothing to rely on for success.

The good news is the Bible provides unchanging principles and wisdom for raising moral, secure, confident and prosperous children.

Interesting

U.S. Department of Justice, Office of Justice Programs
https://www.ojp.gov/pdffiles1/Digitization/140517NCJRS.pdf
(Page i)

"Positive parenting practices during the early years and later in adolescence appear to act as buffers preventing delinquent behavior and assisting adolescents already involved in such behavior in desisting from further delinquency. Research confirms that children raised in supportive, affectionate, and accepting homes are less likely to become deviant. Children rejected by parents are among the most likely to become delinquent."

A Story

People tend to seek the advice of a pastor on many subjects. Thankfully the Bible has lots of answers and principles to follow. I remember one mom weeping and telling me she was at the end of her rope with her 4 year old daughter. Her child would have a temper tantrum if she did not get what she demanded at the local market or store.

I asked the mom how she would respond. The mom replied she would apprehend her kicking and screaming daughter from the shopping cart then leave all her items and just go home. This poor mom was being ruled by her child. She gave up her authority as a parent to a little tiny person. The child knew she was the boss and not her mom. This mom did ultimately apply consistent discipline needed to foster obedience from her child.

(See full story in Parent Tip #15 "Who Runs Your House")

BOTTOM LINE
- You as a parent are given authority by God over your children.
- You must require obedience from your child.
- Your children are seeking guidance and boundaries and need to be led.

Small Group Discussion Questions

What really spoke to you in this "Parent Tip"?

What would you change in your parenting because of this "Parent Tip"?

Do you have any suggestions regarding this "Parent Tip" topic?

Today's Prayer

LORD, help me to be a leader to my children by example and deed. Help me to not waiver in my responsibility as a parent to have proper order in my household, and to raise loving and obedient children with proper respect for authority. In Jesus' Name, I pray. Amen!

Personal Reflection

Parent Tip #6

PRIORITIES, PERSISTENCE, PROTECTION

"Do not be yoked together with unbelievers. For what do righteousness and wickedness have in common? Or what fellowship can light have with darkness?"
2 Corinthians 6:14

Now more than ever children are being influenced and harmed by immoral indoctrination through various television programs, the internet, movies, social media, absurd school curriculum, and other influences. You must be forceful, diligent and persistent in screening and approving not only what enters into your child's soul through their eye and ear gates, but also the amount of time spent watching TV, on social media, their tablets, phones, gaming, etc.

➤ **Know at all times what your child is watching, listening to and doing.**

Whether people believe it or not, there is an agenda to tear down the fabric of Christian moral thought. Protect your child from it! Screen movies and programs through Christian reviews such as the Focus on the Family site - **https://www.pluggedin.com.** Watch things yourself before letting your child watch them or read them. And certainly be careful from whom or what you get your advice and recommendations.

➤ **For sure it is easier to just slap a screen in front of your child as a babysitter.**

But this can hurt their development cognitively, emotionally, socially and spiritually. You must be disciplined as a parent and structured in your approach to dealing with the present tools of society, which are being used ever too frequently and carelessly.

Get educated as to what is beneficial for your child to watch, to play with, to listen to and ingest into their sensitive souls and spirits.

For sure use apps to protect your child from browsing and spending too much time on their pads, phones, and computers. Do not forget you have every right to know what your child is doing. You are the loving, wise and caring authority God has placed in your child's life to protect and guide them.

Outdoor play, acceptable music, reading, playing games, drawing, physical exercise such as swimming, bicycling and sports, are some healthy alternatives to the tube and screen time.

Check out this link for more helpful alternatives. https://kidsbaron.com/blog/alternatives-to-screen-time-for-your-kids

➤ **When it comes to sports and other activities, such as dance and pageantry, you must be cautious.**

Remember all authority figures will have an influence on your child. We hear too many horror stories regarding coaches, scout leaders, and other authority figures, and their improper interaction with children. You must be wise, involved and protective of your child and know who will be influencing them.

Do not let the pressure to conform to this world's patterns or fear to confront cause you to lower your standards as a godly parent.

Pastorally we have found that when an activity interferes with church it can have a detrimental impact upon a child's spirituality and the spiritual health of a family. We never want to give our children the message that God is second to anything. Some parents think their child will become a superstar by committing them to all kinds of sports and activities. Very few do. Fewer than 2 percent of NCAA student-athletes go on to be professional athletes. Ambitions and dreams must be passed by the principles of God's Word, His commandments and much prayer. Worldly success can come with great consequences.

➤ Be careful how and what you choose is best for your child.

Missing church services, youth groups, and involvement in serving in ministry often becomes the norm for those too involved in secular activities. The children get the idea that God is second to what's most important, i.e., being on a sports team, competing in pageants, etc.

This is hard advice for some people to swallow. The teachings of Christ are hard. I am not saying sports, pageants, extra-curricular activities, etc., are inherently evil. But you must be careful to not allow the false gods and the idols of this world to take the place of Christ being the center of your home.

I have never seen families that put extra-curricular activities above the Lord and His Church thrive spiritually.

"But if serving the Lord seems undesirable to you, then choose for yourselves this day whom you will serve, whether the gods your ancestors served beyond the Euphrates, or the gods of the Amorites, in whose land you are living. But as for me and my household, we will serve the Lord." Joshua 24:15

➤ **Moms, be careful putting your little girls in secular dance and pageants.**

Modesty does not seem to be much of a concern these days. Dressing little girls up to look like adults dancing to sensual music is not what your child needs. Also, an overly focused attention on external looks, beauty, self, can lead down a road that leads to great insecurity and self focus. It can also be demeaning and demoralizing. **Look for Christian alternatives.** Keep your children innocent as long as you can.

A Story

Jimmy (fictitious name) loved youth groups and attending church. He was also a natural born athlete. As time went on, sports tournaments began to take up most of his time. It also started taking up the time of the parents. Great family, great kids, but wrong priorities. To make a long story short, coaches became the replacement for youth leaders and pastors; positive Christian peer pressure was taken over by ungodly relationships and worldly role models; the desire for success and scholarships replaced the desire to accomplish the will of God.

A Story (continued)

Not only did the children of this family lose their spiritual way, but the parents did as well and divorce ensued. One of the many sad but true stories of the importance of priorities and making decisions centered around Christ.

Interesting

https://www.soas.ac.uk/gallery/liddell/

"Eric Liddell achieved fame as an Olympic athlete whose life is chronicled in the 1981 film, Chariots of Fire. Liddell's spiritual convictions had a significant impact on his athletic career. As a member of the British Olympic Team for the 1924 Paris Olympic Games, he refused to run in the qualifying heats because they were held on a Sunday, with the consequence that he was forced to withdraw from his best event, the 100 metres race. He went on to win bronze and gold medals in the 200 and 400 metres events respectively, setting a world record for the 400 metres and causing sensational news headlines. In 1925, at the peak of his athletic career, Liddell chose to join the London Missionary Society and went to serve in Northern China."

BOTTOM LINE
- Know what your child is watching and doing at all times.
- Be careful how you set the priorities in your household.
- Always build your child's life around their spirituality.

Small Group Discussion Questions

What really spoke to you in this "Parent Tip"?

What would you change in your parenting because of this "Parent Tip"?

Do you have any suggestions regarding this "Parent Tip" topic?

Today's Prayer

LORD, help me to not conform to this world's patterns and standards. Help me to be attentive, wise and discerning as to what is allowed into my child(ren's) soul and spirit. Help me to be a strong parent willing to make the tough decisions that are best for the emotional and spiritual development of my child(ren). In Jesus' Name, I pray! Amen

Personal Reflection

(Parent Tip #7)

THE IMPORTANCE OF A TALK

About three in the afternoon Jesus cried out in a loud voice, "Eli, Eli, lema sabachthani?" (which means "My God, my God, why have you forsaken me?").
Matthew 27:46

"Let's talk" may be two of the most important words you say to your child(ren). When Jesus was going through His most horrific time, He so longed to hear His Father's voice. The silence of His Father was as grueling as the physical pain He was experiencing. Your child needs to hear your voice even when you are not physically present.

➤ **Take every opportunity to have a conversation with your child.**

Be deliberate about it. It does not have to be a scheduled time, it can be while driving, when eating together, before or after homework time, bedtime, etc. Seize every opportunity to have a talk.

What do you want your child to know? What values do you want your child to have? What experiences and stories do you have that will benefit your child? Ask questions, seek their opinions and feelings about different current events and happenings. Let them feel valued. Ask them why they feel a certain way. Try to understand their view and help them to understand your view and Biblical values. Should they not answer your questions, just keep talking. Tell them how you feel and why. Tell them stories, your stories and Bible stories. Everyone loves to hear a story.

➤ **Every talk is an opportunity to develop friendship, to teach, to listen and learn about your child and for your child to learn about you.**

Sad to say, in the busy world we live in, many children know little about their parent's background, their family's history, the challenges and victories experienced by those closest to them. Talking to your children about your life, the lives of those most closely connected to them gives them a sense of belonging. It helps them to understand they are part of something bigger than just themselves.

The older a child gets the more important it is for them to know they can always talk to their parent(s). Yes, it is true, during adolescence children tend to shut down and would rather speak to someone other than a parent. But this is why it is so important for talks to happen early in a child's life. The more talks the better. The more talks you have about everything, the more your child will hear your voice even when you are not physically speaking to them. They will know exactly what mom and/or dad would say about a particular subject.

➤ **Having talks can unleash many wondrous things about your children you may not know.**

You will get to experience how they think, what they think, what is influencing them, who they look up to, what they like, dislike, the strength of their faith, their unbeliefs, their emotional challenges, their hurts, what brings them happiness, and the list goes on and on.

Your child is absorbing information all day long, at school, from friends, from what they watch and listen to. Someone is talking to them. As a parent you must monitor your child's influences and be the loudest and most influential voice in the room. You must talk regularly to your children. You must make time *and* redeem time to do this.

A Story

Our Senior Pastor, Pastor Stephen Boyce, would always tell stories about his conversations with his children while driving them to school. He would intentionally not put the radio on and use this precious time to talk, become friends with, and influence the developing minds of his children. He encouraged all parents to redeem time to talk with their children. Redeeming time for parenting is crucial to establishing a deep and influential relationship with your children. Do not waste a moment of time that can be used to talk.

Moms usually have an easier time talking with their sons and/or daughters. I know my wife Lori to this day leads the way to making time to talk to our children, and now grandchildren. But it is crucial for dads to do the same. Be intentional about putting away phones, tablets and other distractions. **Just talk!**

Interesting

Throughout my college years I noticed some smart students had difficulty taking tests. They had test anxiety, which is called **testophobia**. So I had determined to find a way to help my children to not be frightened of taking tests when they got older. Our bedtime routine was to read children's books and Bible stories to our children, pray and then put them to bed. Of course as a dad, wrestling would be one of our favorite bedtime activities. My wife did not like that part of our routine, because it was supposed to be a wind down time.

With regards to helping my children not to ever experience testophobia, I figured I would make testing fun. So everytime we finished our bedtime reading, I would tell my children it's time for a talk and test. We would have a fun talk, a review about what we just read. I would then tell them daddy is going to give you a test and ask you questions. Are you ready? They would get so excited and would have some of the funniest answers. One time after talking about how God created man, I asked why did God make skin? One of my children answered with excitement, "to hold your bones in!" You get 100 on your test!

Talk to your children all the time. It is never too late to start.

BOTTOM LINE

- "Let's talk" may be two of the most important words you say to your child.
- Every talk is an opportunity to parent and develop a friendship with your child.
- Talks will let you see into your child's world.

Small Group Discussion Questions

What really spoke to you in this" Parent Tip"?

What would you change in your parenting because of this "Parent Tip"?

Do you have any suggestions regarding this "Parent Tip" topic?

Today's Prayer

LORD, help me to redeem time to talk with my child(ren). Forgive me if I have failed in this area and please help me to make up for lost opportunities. I ask the Holy Spirit to help me to have meaningful conversations with my children and to not ever feel awkward or unable. In Jesus' Name I pray! Amen

Personal Reflection

Parent Tip #8

DECISION MAKING

"Getting wisdom is the wisest thing you can do! And whatever else you do, develop good judgment."
Proverbs 4:7 NLT

➤ **Some parents have a very hands off approach to parenting. Some call it a liberal parenting style.**

Some parents leave many decisions up to their children to make, including daily routines, religious beliefs, church attendance, schooling, friendships, what they watch and read, etc. Some parents believe allowing children to make their own choices is respect for the individual. Other parents are just too busy to be involved in all the decision making required to raise a child. Some parents do not have the energy to deal with the challenge of children who are not compliant.

Although parents need to teach their children how to make good decisions, leaving decision making up to children lacks wisdom and judgment. We call young people children for a reason. They are not adults with the experience needed to make important decisions. A parent must not be lazy in making the best decisions for their children, and or afraid to exercise their authority. A parent must be very involved in making good decisions for their children and acquire the wisdom to do so.

➤ **There are many decisions that need to be made daily for children.**

Your child may choose the type of ice cream they would like to eat, but not decide when they would like to eat it. A child may decide on the color clothing they would like to wear, but not a style of clothing that is inappropriate and lacks modesty.

A child must abide by the rules of the family, including when to eat dinner, bed time, wake time, TV time and programming, homework time, church time, time with friends, etc.

One of the most consequential decisions a parent will make for their child is how they will raise them in **faith** and with a reverence for God. Another important decision is choosing the **friends** a child will keep, and yet another significant decision is determining a child's care and **education.** We will look at these decisions more closely in future "Parent Tips".

➤ **Do not be afraid to make decisions for your children.**

It may be appropriate and beneficial at times to explain and even dialogue with your children regarding your decisions, especially as your child gets older. But an explanation is not always necessary and may even be unwise. For example, if you know it is not safe for your child to go over a certain person's home, no explanation is needed. Your child must trust your judgment and obey your decision. God says a child must obey their parents and that settles it.

"Children, obey your parents in the Lord, for this is right."
Ephesians 6:1

➤ **The challenge for any parent is to go against the flow and to stand firm in their decisions.**

You know how persistent a child can be in trying to get what they want. It is much easier to give in at times. But you owe it to your child to make the right decision and not the easy one. It is more important to be wise than to be liked - for the moment. Remember - *"Getting wisdom is the wisest thing you can do! And whatever else you do, develop good judgment."* Proverbs 4:7 NLT

Lori's Story

There have been many times my husband and I had to make decisions that were contrary to what other parents were making. Living in a neighborhood with other children made it extremely difficult at times to tell our children they could not just do what others were doing. We had our rules and our three children had to obey them.

One rule was never leaving our property without our consent or going into a neighbor's home. We needed to know exactly where our children were at all times, what they were doing and with whom. We would not allow our children to go into someone's home we did not know thoroughly. It did not matter if our neighbors appeared to be nice people and if "all the other kids were there."

Our children along with their friends would try to argue their positions when they disagreed with our decisions.

Lori's Story (continued)

We knew our decisions were based upon wisdom and good judgment. We knew we were responsible to protect our children even when our decisions were not liked by them.

Sometimes my husband and I would disagree on decisions regarding our children. I was more protective than him. He would sometimes tell me, "boys need to be boys." But we did our best to not disagree in front of our children and to come to mutual agreement on our parenting decisions.

Being in unity as parents is very important. Your decisions should be based upon the Word of God, prayer, and wisdom. Do not be hesitant to seek counsel from godly leaders who have good fruit in their lives when it comes to raising children. Your decisions will greatly impact your children.

Even when your children enter their older teen years, you must provide wisdom in making decisions. When my daughter Carissa was nineteen, she was invited to a summer mission program in Belisle. My husband and I were feeling uneasy because she would not be in the care of anyone we knew. We prayed about it often but could not get a sense of peace.

Two weeks before Carissa was going to depart for the trip, she received an itinerary of the trip's daily schedule. The mission organization instructed her to wear an identifiable T-shirt and wait outside the airport for transportation.

Lori's Story (continued)

She was also instructed, if no one shows up go to the business across from the airport to phone the organization. This was unacceptable to us. Asking a young girl to hope for transportation was unprofessional and not secure. This led to us making a hard decision. We asked our daughter to cancel the trip.

Many tears were shed, back and forth conversation was had, and we even sought pastoral counsel. Ultimately Carissa obeyed our decision, even at nineteen. We had earned her trust over the years.

The very night Carissa canceled the trip, her close friend invited her to another mission trip. This time it was to Guatemala and there were chaperones we knew and trusted. It was the same time frame as her other trip. God has a way of backing you as a loving parent. He hears your prayers, and He also knows your child's desires. Carissa has now completed eight mission trips as she loves caring for children.

BOTTOM LINE
- Get wisdom for your parenting decisions.
- Do not be afraid to make decisions for your children.
- It is more important to be wise than to be liked.

Small Group Discussion Questions

What really spoke to you in this "Parent Tip"?

What would you change in your parenting because of this "Parent Tip"?

Do you have any suggestions regarding this "Parent Tip" topic?

Today's Prayer

LORD, help me to make wise decisions for my children and to not be influenced by this world and its pressure to conform. Make me strong in my resolve to lead my children well and to not become weary when challenged. In Jesus' Name I pray, Amen!

Personal Reflection

Parent Tip #9

ENGINEERING FRIENDSHIPS

Do not be misled: "Bad company corrupts good character." 1 Corinthians 15:33

The Bible clearly instructs us to not be misled when it comes to choosing the company we keep. No one should consider themselves strong enough to be in close relationship with those involved in a sinful lifestyle, and those who would place them in a compromising spiritual position and environment. This pertains to adults and parents first, and then of course to children.

Peer pressure affects all age groups. Thus, the engineering of friendships is crucial to everyone's spiritual, emotional, psychological and even physical well-being.

> **It starts with parents. Everything you do, and what and who you allow into your life and home will affect you and your children.**

You must protect yourself and your children from relationships that will bring temptation and spiritual decline into your home. The Bible does not mince words when it comes to relationships. We read in *2 Corinthians 6:14*,

"Do not be yoked together with unbelievers. For what do righteousness and wickedness have in common? Or what fellowship can light have with darkness?"

The people you associate with as a parent will have a spiritual impact upon you and your children. This world is spiritual and the Bible tells us to not fellowship with darkness.

So the godliness of your friendships and who you allow into the sanctity of your home must be carefully examined. Do not expect your children to have healthy friendships if you are not leading the way.

"Follow my example, as I follow the example of Christ."
1 Corinthians 11:1

As believers we are called to love the unlovely, minister to the hurting, and bring Christ to the lost. But we are not called to throw out wisdom and to allow godlessness into our relationships and homes.

➤ **It is critical for a parent to engineer their child(ren)'s friendships.**

One definition of the word engineer is to *skillfully or artfully arrange for (an event or situation) to occur*. Parenting is not an easy job. It takes quite a bit of engineering, skillfully and artfully arranging for your child to have a blessed life, which requires healthy friendships.

You cannot leave your child's friendships up to happenstance, to whoever they meet in school, in the neighborhood and even in church. There are times when even family members may not be who you want influencing your child. You want your child to have friends that will not bring harm to them in any way, and especially spiritually. This means you have to be wise in helping them to foster godly relationships.

➤ As a parent you have to operate as a detective.

Like a detective you need to do some behind the scenes investigating of your child's relationships, and adjust accordingly. Do your due diligence. You want to encourage some friendships and discourage or outright reject others. Your children do not need to know you are helping to choose their friends. Be wise, discreet and careful in how you discuss and address their relationships.

When our children were young we searched for godly families with children of their age. This usually happened in church. There is no better place to help your children make good friends than in a local church. Children and youth ministry are where it's at! But even so, we were very careful with the choices we made, and we engineered the amount of time our children spent with friends, where they met, what they were doing, and what oversight they had. We worked hard at engineering their relationships.

➤ Battles may ensue.

When our children became youth, there were times when battles ensued as to our requirements and standards, such as never missing church youth groups, and with who, where and when they were allowed to hang out. Of course, even our children had to come into their own relationship with Christ, and deal with sin, disobedience, rebellion and failure.

But this does not let us off the hook as parents in providing clear direction, commands, reprimand and initiating consequence. We are responsible to God to be good parents and our children are responsible to God to obey their parents.

A Story

Our children did not know we would ask certain older young people to help us spiritually influence them. We wanted them to have good mentors and role models in their lives and we realized young people listen to other young people. We would ask certain youth to take our children out with them and, of course, we would pay and pray the way. We would also ask our young mentors to speak into our children's lives and help them to see spirituality and coolness are one and the same.

Having older young people involved in our children's lives created opportunities for them to discuss their feelings, fears, faith, unbeliefs, likes and dislikes. Sometimes our children even complained about their parents' strictness. That was Ok with my wife and I because we wanted our children to be honest with their feelings. We considered it a benefit to have them vent to a young believer who we trusted would give them godly insight and advice.

Lori's Story

When I was 16, my best friend began dating a guy from High School. During this time she was not making good choices. My friend never did anything wrong when she was with me but with her boyfriend, she did whatever he did. He was an extremely bad influence on her. I tried to speak truth to her, but she would not listen.

One day I came home from school and my family sat me down and asked me a serious question; "Does your friend drink?" They said "You better not lie to us, tell us the truth". I told them that she never drank in front of me just when she was with her boyfriend. Their answer to that was, "From this day forward you will never get in a car with her again!" I was devastated. She was my best friend for many years. I did not know that my family called her family and told them their concern for their daughter. They were very angry and accused us all of lying about their daughter. "My daughter would never do any of those things they said."

My friend never spoke to me again, and that was the end of our friendship. I look back now and thank God for my family's protection over me. It was a hard stand to take, but they loved me enough to not have me in the car with someone who drinks. My safety took priority over my friendship.

Peer pressure is more powerful than parenting at some stages of your child's development. You must search for peers you know will be a good influence on your children. This takes work, wisdom and engineering of their relationships.

Interesting

Taken from: *https://headsup.scholastic.com/students/peer-pressure-its-influence-on-teens-and-decision-making/*

"According to Dr. B. J. Casey from the Weill Medical College of Cornell University, teens are very quick and accurate in making judgments and decisions on their own and in situations where they have time to think. However, when they have to make decisions in the heat of the moment or in social situations, their decisions are often influenced by external factors like peers. In a study funded by the National Institute on Drug Abuse (NIDA), teen volunteers played a video driving game, either alone or with friends watching. What the researchers discovered was that the number of risks teens took in the driving game more than doubled when their friends were watching as compared to when the teens played the game alone. This outcome indicates that teens may find it more difficult to control impulsive or risky behaviors when their friends are around, or in situations that are emotionally charged."

BOTTOM LINE
- Everything you do as a parent will affect your children.
- You must engineer your child(ren)'s friendships.
- Parents must be detectives.
- Having battles with your children is normal.

Small Group Discussion Questions

What really spoke to you in this "Parent Tip"?

What would you change in your parenting because of this "Parent Tip"?

Do you have any suggestions regarding this "Parent Tip" topic?

Today's Prayer

LORD, guide me in helping my children and me develop healthy godly relationships that will benefit our lives. Provide me with discernment, strength and wisdom in doing what is best for my family. Even when things get heated, please help me to stand my ground and make decisions backed by your Word, blessing and support. In Jesus' Name I pray, Amen!

Personal Reflection

Parent Tip #10

MAKING MEMORIES

"I thank my God in all my remembrance of you."
Philippians 1:3

Some of the greatest stories we have in life come from memories created by our own experiences. Making positive memories with our children is what they will carry into adulthood. These memories will birth feelings of joy, love and closeness. *Memories are the fabric of life and family.*

Someone said; "Sometimes small memories cover large parts of our hearts." Sad to say, some memories you would rather forget. They are too painful to relive. Memories are powerful, thus, it is extremely important to have more good memories than bad.

➤ **You want your children to have good memories. It is up to you to create them.**

Moments of fun, closeness, laughter, spirituality and even sharing sorrow together, is what creates memories. There are seven days in a week, with twenty four hours in each day. It is so important to evaluate the amount of time spent with each of your children, and even more important, how you spend time with them. Unless you grab hold of time, it will quickly vanish and be consumed by mundane tasks, inconsequential activity, and lost opportunity for lasting memories.

➤ **You must be thoughtful in how you spend time with your children and what you desire for them to remember and carry into their future.**

The best memories are formed by moments of heartfelt connection with those you love. A child's healthy and consequential memories are often built on a foundation of love and devoted time together with family. Thus, a parent must devote time to create memories.

Whether it is a simple weekly talk, walk or drive to your child's favorite candy shop, ice cream parlor, park, toy store, clothing store, library, etc., or an annual vacation with the family, you are creating memories. It is never too late to create moments your children will remember forever. It just takes deliberate and consistent action.

Lori's Story

I grew up being raised by my sister and brother-in-law from the age of five. My mom died when I was two years of age and my dad passed away when I was eleven. I had also lost my older brother in a car accident when I was eight years old. I was in the car with him when it happened. Needless to say, I had lots of traumatic memories. But these memories did not consume me or define me because they were overtaken by many more good memories and my relationship with the Lord.

Lori's Story (continued)

Looking back over my life I give thanks for the happy memories created by my sister and brother-in-law. First of all they loved me as their own child, and they spent much time with their two children, who I see as my sisters, and me.

Every Sunday we would go to church together and then go out to eat at one of our favorite restaurants. This was a weekly ritual that blessed me tremendously. Not only did this time create a spiritual bond within my family, but it provided an opportunity to talk and relate to something we shared in common, our faith. Of course being able to order anything I wanted at the local restaraunt was an added bonus and cherished memory. Just being together as a family meant the world to me. It brought great security into my life.

Also, every year we went on a family vacation. We visited many places, but most of my memories from these trips are filled with the feeling of closeness as a family. The losses I experienced as a child were healed by the new memories created by my family.

My husband and I have developed the same kind of memories with our children by being deliberate and consistent in making fun and memorable times with them. Going to church weekly, family dinners, vacations and walks to the ice cream parlor, are memories all three of my children cherish. Good memories help mold good character.

BOTTOM LINE
- Memories are powerful and form the fabric of life and family.
- You must grab hold of time to create special moments with your children.
- It's up to you as a parent to create good memories.
- Good memories help mold good character.

Small Group Discussion Questions

What really spoke to you in this "Parent Tip"?

What would you change in your parenting because of this "Parent Tip"?

Do you have any suggestions regarding this "Parent Tip" topic?

Today's Prayer

LORD, help me to evaluate the time spent with my children and give me wisdom in creating lasting positive memories with them. Help me to prioritize wisely and not waste time doing inconsequential tasks. May my children's lives be filled with memories that will help them be spiritually and emotionally healthy people. In Jesus' Name I pray, Amen!

Personal Reflection

(Parent Tip #11)

SEXUALITY: When and How

"I praise you because I am fearfully and wonderfully made; your works are wonderful, I know that full well."
Psalm 139:14

We are created by God as sexual beings to procreate and to experience pleasure in the sacredness of marriage. So it is only normal for a child to explore their bodies at a young age. A parent's role in helping a child to understand their feelings when it comes to sexuality is an important aspect of parenting. It is critical to teach your child what is acceptable and not acceptable behavior.

> **The problem for some parents is they do not feel comfortable talking to their child about their sexuality.**

If you as a parent do not teach your child and guide, adjust and modify your child's behavior, someone else will. You do not want your child being influenced, confused, indoctrinated and molded by the world's definitions of acceptable sexual behavior and gender identity. As you know, there is sexual messaging everywhere vying for your child's body, soul and spirit. Our role as parents is to give our children a Biblical roadmap to a healthy, godly, and beneficial Christian lifestyle.

> **You cannot let your guard down as a parent.**

You have to protect your child's developing mind. Otherwise, it will be developed by cultural thought as heard and seen through television programming, commercials, movies, books, social media, music, influencers, public school classrooms and even godless friends, family members and neighbors.

"Because of this, God gave them over to shameful lusts. Even their women exchanged natural sexual relations for unnatural ones. In the same way the men also abandoned natural relations with women and were inflamed with lust for one another. Men committed shameful acts with other men, and received in themselves the due penalty for their error." Romans 1:26-27

- **When a child is very young, ages 3 to 5 years old, your responsibility is to teach basic boundaries.**

A child needs to know it is not appropriate to play with their genitals nor should anyone ever touch their private parts. A child should always be told that no one is to see or touch their privates or ask them to undress. They should also be told to tell mom and or dad should anyone ever get too close to them and touch them where they should not - no matter who it is! And if someone says, do not tell mom or dad, they are not to listen. Teach your children early on about modesty and it is not ok to see any adults and peers with no clothing on.

- **Provide information gradually as you see questions arising, situations presenting, and the Holy Spirit nudging.**

Your 4 year old is likely not thinking about reproduction, sexuality, gender identity and all this world is throwing at children. But your 8 to 10 year old child may be getting more exposed to these topics than you think.

Thus, you have to be attentive to your role as the ultimate teacher and guide in your child's life.

➤ **There is no exact age for explaining God's creation of male and female, how they function physically, how a child is made and born, etc.**

You just need to know it is important to not give over this responsibility to anyone else. Do not hold off when you know it is time for a conversation. You do not need to discuss every topic on sexuality in one sitting, but you must do so over time. Always be willing to answer any questions your child may ask, no matter how difficult and or uncomfortable. Your child needs you.

Take some time to research some good Christian reading material on the topic of discussing sexuality with your children. Organizations such as Focus on the Family are very helpful in providing resources for Christian parents.

BOTTOM LINE
- Overcome not feeling comfortable discussing sexuality with your children.
- You are responsible for parenting your children's sexuality.
- Start with discussing basic boundaries when children are very young, then all topics and questions as they grow older.

Small Group Discussion Questions

What really spoke to you in this "Parent Tip"?

What would you change in your parenting because of this "Parent Tip"?

Do you have any suggestions regarding this "Parent Tip" topic?

Today's Prayer

LORD, protect my children from developing an unhealthy view of their sexuality. Help me to be wise and deliberate in guiding them along the way in understanding God's design for their lives. In Jesus' Name I pray, Amen!

Personal Reflection

Parent Tip #12

STRONG-WILLED CHILDREN

"This is what the Lord Almighty, the God of Israel, says: Go and tell the people of Judah and those living in Jerusalem, 'Will you not learn a lesson and obey my words?' declares the Lord." Jeremiah 35:12

When we look at Biblical history we see even God had to deal with strong willed people. We read stories in the Old Testament of God losing patience and wanting to just wipe everyone out. Not unlike what a parent feels like at times. But we know grace won out. Thank God!

> **Many parents walk around with a burden of guilt and shame.**

Some parents feel like they are failing because of the challenges of dealing with the attitude and behavior of a strong-willed child. This is not uncommon. Many families have a strong-willed child.

Compliant children tend to conform and follow family rules. They ultimately obey and can be directed with ease. Not that compliant children are perfect, but for sure they are more easily instructed, disciplined and molded by their parents.

But then there is the other child! The strong-willed child is like a metal bar that takes quite a bit of heat and strength to bend. This can cause extreme pressure, frustration and angst on a parent. A strong-willed child can leave a parent feeling guilty and inept and saying things such as: "What am I doing wrong? I am not a good parent. I do not know how to handle this child! I cannot take this anymore! What should I do?"

➤ What do you do with a strong-willed child?

One thing for certain, do not give up! A parent must do all he or she can to live by the scriptural principles of parenting with every child, no matter how challenging at times. A parent must continue to love deeply, instruct, communicate, discipline, seek help, pray, and apply wisdom in every situation with every child, compliant and strong-willed.

Do not ever give up your authority as a parent. Do not stop applying consistency in training and disciplining, and do not allow animosity to come between you and your strong-willed child. It is also important to not let a strong-willed child bring dissension between you and your spouse. Stay in unity and know your parenting, consistency and prayer will ultimately produce good fruit.

➤ God is involved in your child's life.

Sometimes parenting is more about praying than anything else. There are times when you just have to give your child over to the Lord. When things do not appear to be working, you have to go to God. Only God can do what you cannot do in winning over your children to Him, to you as their parent, to protecting them, and leading them on the proper path. God can do what you cannot do!

A Story

Every one of our three children had unique temperaments. One of them was the most active and at times a handful. Even at a young age, our main job became keeping him safe and alive. He would climb out of his crib and crawl down the stairs to the first level. He would somehow get out of his car seat while we were traveling. We called him *Houdini*, after the famous escape artist. We had to secure his ankles together while in his car seat for his own protection. He would even escape the house through the front door and end up across the street in a neighbor's yard. Even when latched he would drag a chair to climb upon and unlatch the door. I can go on and on. Needless to say, he required a lot of energy, prayer, grace and consistency. He was in no way an easy child. But as said in a former "Parent Tip", there is no such thing as a bad child.

To top things off, my second son had seizures as a child. It started when he was 9 months old. He literally would stop breathing as we waited for paramedics to come to the rescue. This was when we had to learn to trust God with our children. The fear of dealing with a child with seizures took a toll on our emotional and even physical health as a family. We would ask God, "Why was this happening to our child, to our family? What did we do wrong?" This is a whole other topic. Our only solution was to pray and trust God and get prayer and support from people God has put in your life. When you do not know what else to do in any situation, you must give it to God and ask Him to do what you cannot do.

Interesting

Some of the greatest works on Christian parenting are by Dr. James Dobson. The New Strong-Willed Child by Dr. Dobson is a book every parent of a strong-willed child should have. Dare to Discipline is another great book.

Also, here is a helpful PDF from The Parenting Center with some practical tips on parenting a strong-willed child.

https://www.esc16.net/upload/page/0307/docs/Stevenson%20The%20Strong%20Willed%20Child.pdf

BOTTOM LINE
- Do not let feelings of failure overtake you as a parent. Keep parenting!
- Many families have both compliant and strong-willed children. You are not alone.
- Do not forget to go to God when it seems like your parenting is not working out.

Small Group Discussion Questions

What really spoke to you in this "Parent Tip"?

What would you change in your parenting because of this "Parent Tip"?

Do you have any suggestions regarding this "Parent Tip" topic?

Today's Prayer

LORD, help me to understand you create every child as a unique being with strengths, weaknesses, gifts and talents. Help me to see all my children through your eyes and give me the love, strength, wisdom and persistence to shape and mold each of them into who you want them to be. In Jesus' Name I pray, Amen!

Personal Reflection

Parent Tip #13

DAYCARE AND EDUCATION

"Train up a child in the way he should go: and when he is old, he will not depart from it."
Proverbs 22:6

Every aspect of a child's life is influenced by external factors, including daycare and education. Most students in America spend about 1,260 hours a year in school, which is based upon 180 school days and 7 hours of schooling per day. This is a significant and transformative amount of time, either for the good or the bad.

➤ **A child will be deeply impacted by who is caring and educating them, and by what they are being taught.**

The Bible says, train up a child in the way he (or she) should go. This means there is a proper way to train a child. We know that this way is following the teachings of scripture. There are other godless ways to raise children, and we can see the great harm those ways are bringing to children, youth and society. This leads a parent to having to make very wise and careful decisions regarding babysitting, daycare, homeschooling, public or private education, college, trade school, etc.

➤ **Is daycare the only solution?**

The Pew Research Center reports 46 percent of American families now have both parents working full time, up from 31 percent in 1970. Twenty-six percent of families have a working dad and a stay-at-home mom, down from 46 percent 45 years ago. This means 74% of families now have working moms. This shift in less parents being home with their children during daytime hours leads to another statistic.

According to estimates from the National Household Education Survey, 58% of working parents with children five years old and younger, or about 6.38 million parents in the US use center-based child care options.

Statistics show more and more families have two parents working and nearly 60% of families use daycare centers. There are various reasons why people use daycares. The high cost of living is one of them, and being a single parent is another. But the use of a daycare is not always the best or wisest solution for the caring of children.

As a pastor and former banker I have sat with many families to discuss finances and the cost of daycare. It is amazing how many families were better off having a parent stay at home to care for their children versus paying for daycare. When you crunch the numbers, the cost of daycare and associated expenses, such as transportation, work clothing, an increase in income taxes, food, coffee, parking fees, etc., often outweighs the financial benefit of having two parents working. Another consideration is the impact of taking a child out of a safe, healthy and nurturing home environment and putting them into a daycare business that may not have the best of ethics and care. A daycare should be the last choice and not the first, and with much study and parental oversight.

- **God understands the challenges faced by parents in the care of their young children.**

Weigh out your options to determine what is best for your child first, then yourself second. Pray and ask the Lord, spiritual leaders and parents for advice and guidance when making decisions regarding care and education for your child.

Some parents cannot stand being at home all day long with children and would rather work. They may even feel as though they are healthier parents by providing themselves a reprieve from all day parenting. This is understandable. Being an at home parent is the hardest job in the world, but also the most important and rewarding. The decisions made regarding the care of your children must be done with much prayer and consideration. You always want what is best for your children.

- **Education - As your child gets older you will need to determine how and where to educate them.**

Now more than ever, making the right decision as to the education of your child is more crucial than ever. Your child's spiritual and emotional well being is greatly impacted by their schooling. Depending upon your community and your child's temperment your options may be limited.

Sad to say public education may no longer be a viable choice for people of faith, especially in certain areas of our nation.

All the work, prayer and parenting you do at home and at church may be undone by an environment that is hostile to Biblical values, teachings and the Christian lifestyle.

➤ **Not many children can withstand a constant bombardment against their moral values and religious beliefs.**

"But mark this: There will be terrible times in the last days. People will be lovers of themselves, lovers of money, boastful, proud, abusive, disobedient to their parents, ungrateful, unholy, without love, unforgiving, slanderous, without self-control, brutal, not lovers of the good, treacherous, rash, conceited, lovers of pleasure rather than lovers of God— having a form of godliness but denying its power. Have nothing to do with such people." 2 Timothy 3:1-5

In addition to having to deal with godless ideology in the public school system, students are sometimes challenged by authority combative to their faith. Immoral peer pressure is also a constant. Christian children can often feel like sheep among wolves in a place that is supposed to provide a positive learning experience. We are living in what the Bible calls *terrible times* and a parent must remember God gives them the responsibility to protect their children.

➤ **So what does a parent do?**

Some parents are doing all they can to send their children to private religious schools. Others are joining the homeschool movement. As of February 2020, at least 9 million Americans had gone through homeschooling at least once.

From 2019 to the fall of 2020, the percentage of homeschooled students changed from 3.4% to 9%.

My wife and I drove old cars, ate at home versus restaurants, and watched our expenses very closely in order to afford sending our children to Christian schools. It was worth the sacrifice and investment. Christian education certainly helped mold who our children have become as successful faith-filled adults.

➤ **God knows the situation of every family regarding the care and education of their children.**

Even in less desirable circumstances, with God's help, hard work, wisdom, parental involvement and constant oversight and input, a parent can raise successful godly children. Whatever the age and or spiritual condition of your child, do not give up. Keep parenting!

A Story

It was not easy going from being a Bank Vice President with a big salary and expense account to a church staff salary. Many people advised me against leaving my business career for full time ministry. But I knew it was the calling of God upon my life and family. My wife and I would have to learn to put our faith and trust in God for all our needs.

A Story (continued)

When we had our children, we had to make a decision as to our income stream. Even though my wife's job provided a second source of income for our family, it did not allow her to be at home with the kids. We prayed and decided to establish an at home daycare business. This would allow my wife to care for our children and bring in much needed income. For twelve years my wife cared for one or two other children in addition to our three. For our family this was the right decision, especially considering there were no Christian care alternatives.

Always pray for God to provide you with the best solutions for the care of your children. Do not panic, be unwise, settle for easy versus what's best. Your child is way too important to not do your due diligence when it comes to their care and education.

BOTTOM LINE
- A child will be deeply impacted by their care and education.
- Daycare is an option, but not always the only or best option.
- Not many children can do well in a public school setting.
- God knows your situation and will help you.

Small Group Discussion Questions

What really spoke to you in this "Parent Tip"?

What would you change in your parenting because of this "Parent Tip"?

Do you have any suggestions regarding this "Parent Tip" topic?

Today's Prayer

LORD, you know I want the best for my children. Please grant me the strength, resources and wisdom to make right decisions regarding their personal care and education. Please protect my children from the false gods of this world and let them have a personal experience with you that will guide them into your plans for their lives. In Jesus' Name, I pray. Amen!

Personal Reflection

(Parent Tip #14)

YES, NO, MAYBE

"All you need to say is simply 'Yes' or 'No' anything beyond this comes from the evil one."
Matthew 5:37

Have you ever said yes, when you should have said no, or no when you should have said yes or maybe? We all have. We can all look back and see incorrect decisions made by haste, lack of judgment or by an answer of convenience. Hindsight is 20/20.

➤ **What can you learn from past mistakes regarding your children?**

What can you learn from saying yes, when it should have been no, or no when it should have been maybe or yes? The bottom line is, decisions should be based upon much thought, prayer, concrete principles and rules and sticktoitiveness.

Your children will be asking you questions throughout most of their lives. Their questions may mature from may I have candy to may I borrow money? But needless to say, you still have to answer yes, no, or maybe, and your response may be detrimental to your child's well-being. So think before you speak!

➤ **When a child is young, due to peer pressure, he or she may be looking for you to be their fall guy.**

It is hard for a young person to oppose peer pressure. Your saying no can make it easier for them to not go against their conscience and better judgment. "No" can be the most positive and beneficial response you make for your child. Your strong, *wise decisions bring security!

➤ **Learn how to soften your no. Say no without saying no.**

Provide options for your children. You may not want them going to see a certain movie, but another movie may be fine. You may not want them over a certain person's house, but they may all come over to your house. Make food!

Before saying no, respond by saying, have you thought about ....? You may have a better time doing ...., or, let me think and pray about it, etc. You do not always have to provide a dissertation for your responses, but your children need to know you are not just winging it, and are looking out for their best interests.

➤ Some important guidelines to follow regarding how to answer your child's requests are as follows.

1. Do not be pressured or coerced into answering on your child's timeline or succumbing to their emotional response.
2. Take time to make a decision so you can answer wisely. It is ok to say "maybe" to allow yourself to think about things, seek godly wisdom, pray and make the right decision.
3. "No" is not a bad word, but saying no and doing the opposite is not beneficial to your child gaining confidence in your decisions.
4. Explain the whys behind your rules. They need to know you are making decisions for their best interests and not just for convenience.
5. Requests should always be made directly to you as a parent without any other influences around, like friends and other family members. (The answer to our children's requests would always be no when asked in front of their friends.)
6. Your children don't have to agree with your decision, they only have to Obey. They will never fully understand the WHY in your decision until they are parents themselves. We see this now since our children are grown with kids of their own. They have thanked us for protecting them and holding firm to our beliefs.

BOTTOM LINE
- A parent must know the reasons behind their yes, no and maybe.
- A child finds security in parents making right decisions for them.
- You can learn how to say no without coming across as uncaring.
- Set up guidelines for answering your children's requests.

Small Group Discussion Questions

What really spoke to you in this "Parent Tip"?

What would you change in your parenting because of this "Parent Tip"?

Do you have any suggestions regarding this "Parent Tip" topic?

Today's Prayer

LORD, help me to not be double minded in my parenting. Give me wisdom in making right decisions regarding my children's requests and make me strong in my resolve. In Jesus' Name, I pray. Amen!

Personal Reflection

Parent Tip #15

WHO RUNS YOUR HOUSE

"Whoever spares the rod hates their children, but the one who loves their children is careful to discipline them."
Proverbs 13:24

The topic of discipline can be a sensitive and confusing one for various reasons. Sometimes personal experiences with abusive discipline can lead a parent to shy away from the necessity of proper discipline. Also, the ever changing teachings of this world's culture and institutions can often contradict the teachings of scripture. This causes many parents to not know who to turn to for answers. As with all our "Parent Tips" we seek guidance and solutions from the Bible.

> **The Bible clearly teaches children must obey their parents, which means parents must be able to direct their children.**

"...because the Lord disciplines the one he loves, and he chastens everyone he accepts as his son." Hebrews 12:6

There is much confusion surrounding the subject of discipline. Some people believe there is never a justification for spanking a child. Spanking is often confused with child abuse. For sure spanking should never be done in anger and should never be abusive. But what does a parent do when all else fails when a child is in complete rebellion?

> **Rebellion is a willful defiance towards a parent's authority.**

When a child says "no" or just walks away from a parent's commands, that is active rebellion. Some children just throw a temper tantrum in active opposition to a parent's commands.

A child can also display passive rebellion by just not doing what he or she is asked to do, no matter how many times asked or how asked. Or a child decides the parent's instruction is not how they will do things, If they do comply it will be on their timeline and terms. This is passive rebellion.

> **The Bible is quite clear that rebellion against a parent's authority should not be tolerated.**

Rebellion is a form of control. There must be consequences.

For sure it takes a lot of work to deal with a child's improper behavior and especially when a child has a strong will. But this is a parent's job, and a child's character development is dependent upon their obedience. A child's will must submit to a parent's will. ***This is divine order.***

It is much easier to develop a child when younger than older. The longer you wait to require a child to obey instruction the harder it gets. Bad habit patterns develop when discipline in the home is inept, scarce or wrongly implemented.

"Children, obey your parents in the Lord, for this is right."
Ephesians 6:1

▶ Manipulation is not proper discipline.

Some parents resort to manipulation rather than teaching the rules and requirements of the home. Using a child's carnal desires to get a proper response is not discipline. Appealing to covetousness, trickery, intimidation, playing on a child's emotions and desires will not develop an obedient heart. You should have set rules and clear consequences. If your child willfully disobeys an understood command, you do not want to negotiate obedience. You should never allow your child to make a reward a requirement for obedience. "I will obey only if you give me candy." This puts the child in control and not the parent. Nor do you need to always provide incentive for obedience. For example; "If you obey, then I will take you for ice cream." The proper response for disobedience should be justice, i.e., "you know the consequence for disobeying." Of course acknowledge and affirm a child's obedience. There is nothing wrong with rewarding a child for good behavior.

When a child is rebellious, redirecting disobedience to a more acceptable activity is not good discipline. Redirecting behavior is OK, but not when there is outright refusal to obey a parent.

▶ You know it's time to work on discipline when kids rule.

When a parent no longer has control over bed time, what and when children eat, watch on TV, time spent on tablets and phones, how they dress and respond to requirements of the home, etc., the house is out of order. Parents no longer have the authority, their words have become mere suggestions.

It's time to regain authority through prayer, wisdom, clear rules, much conversation, and consequences. A parent's will must be stronger than a child's will.

➤ Is it ever proper to spank a child?

Every parent needs to honestly assess their methods of discipline and its results. Some children are more easily led than others. What works for one may not work for another. What's important is developing children who are obedient and display Christlike character and not a spirit of rebellion. Rebellion should never be tolerated. A parent must figure out the best method of discipline to eliminate it in the home. Manipulation is not a good method as it only appeals to the carnal nature of the child. The Bible is quite clear discipline may require the rod of correction.

A parent must establish or reestablish divine order in the home. It can be done and it is absolutely necessary. A child who has permissive parents can end up suffering with anxiety because it causes the child to have to make adult decisions.

A Story

Years ago a woman in our church came up to me weeping about her uncontrollable 4 year old child. She said she can no longer go shopping because her child screams bloody murder if she does not get what she wants in the store. Sometimes she would give in, but then her daughter would want something else and the tantrum would begin again. I asked her how she would handle the situation. The lady told me she yells and threatens the child with taking away her toys, but the child does not listen. She ends up leaving the store frustrated, embarrassed and angry.

We prayed about the situation and asked God for wisdom and strength for mom. I asked her if she had ever considered taking the child to her car and giving her a little spank. First explain to your child what was going to happen and why. Then let the child know how much mom loves her and she is a good girl. After the discipline, go back into the store and shop. If this act does not work the first time, do it again. Needless to say, mom comes up to me weeks later and says she cannot believe the difference in her child's behavior.

A parent cannot let a child rule. This is detrimental to the child's well being and to the peace of God in the home. Repentance and change is a Biblical command in the life of a believer, young and old.

BOTTOM LINE
- Children must obey their parents.
- Manipulation is not discipline.
- You must find a method of discipline that works.

Small Group Discussion Questions

What really spoke to you in this "Parent Tip"?

What would you change in your parenting because of this "Parent Tip"?

Do you have any suggestions regarding this "Parent Tip" topic?

Today's Prayer

LORD, give me patience and understanding needed to properly discipline my children in love. Help me to maintain godly order and peace in my home to foster the maturing of spiritually and emotionally healthy children. In Jesus' Name, I pray. Amen!

Personal Reflection

Parent Tip #16

BIG EARS

"We demolish arguments and every pretension that sets itself up against the knowledge of God, and we take captive every thought to make it obedient to Christ."
2 Corinthians 10:5

Have you noticed how children have big ears? It is amazing how your children will hear everything you say as a parent, which means they are hearing everything around them. The thought processes of a child are being developed at a very young age by the information going into their ears and eyes, the windows to their souls. A parent's job is to ensure it is quality input that brings life and spiritual health.

- **The Bible tells us to take every thought captive that is contrary to Christ.**

Depending on the age of a child, the ability to filter out harmful thoughts that come from what they see and hear is not easy. Therefore, it is a parent's role to carefully protect a child and to ensure what they are seeing and hearing is not creating harmful thoughts contrary to Christ. Nothing is more beneficial or harmful to a child than what they hear and see modeled in the home by parents who they expect and need to be role models.

- **Do not expect your child to not be influenced by what they hear and see in the house.**

The home is supposed to be a sanctuary of love, peace, and safety. Now more than ever, a child needs to feel safe in his or her own home. The saying, "garbage in, garbage out" is a saying used to express the idea that in computing and other spheres, incorrect or poor quality input will always produce faulty output. There is great truth to this saying.

How you conduct yourself around your child, your behavior, your speech, your reaction to circumstances, your relationship with your spouse, friends, and family is being absorbed into your child's brain, emotions and spirit. They will often repeat what is heard at home. You often hear a child say, my mommy said, or my daddy said…

Even into adulthood a child will carry with them their experiences as a child. There is nothing more important to a child's well being than what they receive at home from a parent, and their experiences with people who are supposed to be protective and caring agents in their lives.

➤ **It is much easier for a child to grow into a healthy adult when they have healthy adult parents at home.**

You as a parent must be very attentive to your speech and actions, for they are fashioning your children. Your child is watching you, listening to you, absorbing and reacting to what they receive from you. They will emulate what they believe is normal. You as a parent are creating their *normal*. Children will even grow up looking for a mate like their mom or dad.

➤ **If you had a video recording your speech and actions at home would you be proud or embarrassed.**

Even though no one is perfect, would the atmosphere being created at home be considered healthy for your children or harmful.

If you did not have a healthy experience in your home as a child, do not repeat the bad behavior. Pass on the legacy of Christ to your children!

"If anyone causes one of these little ones—those who believe in me—to stumble, it would be better for them to have a large millstone hung around their neck and to be drowned in the depths of the sea. Woe to the world because of the things that cause people to stumble!"
Matthew 18:6-7

Interesting

According to Andrew Newberg, M.D. and Mark Waldman, the authors of *Words Can Change Your Brain*, positive words, "can alter the expression of genes, strengthening areas in our frontal lobes and promoting the brain's cognitive functioning."

BOTTOM LINE

- Your children are being fashioned by what they see and hear at home.
- Children need healthy parents feeding them healthy input.
- Do what it takes to provide a wholesome home environment.

Small Group Discussion Questions

What really spoke to you in this "Parent Tip"?

What would you change in your parenting because of this "Parent Tip"?

Do you have any suggestions regarding this "Parent Tip" topic?

Today's Prayer

LORD, help me to create a home environment that provides love, safety and peace for my children. Deliver and heal me from anything that may be harmful to my emotional and spiritual well- being and to my children. In Jesus' Name, I pray. Amen!

Personal Reflection

(Parent Tip #17)

HAPPINESS IS NOT THE GOAL

"When Jesus had finished saying these things, the crowds were amazed at his teaching, because he taught as one who had authority, and not as their teachers of the law."
Matthew 7:28-29

Jesus was compassionate, caring, kind, gracious, giving and sacrificial. Yet Jesus was unbending in His convictions and spoke with full authority. He was just and strong. He was not looking for acceptance, or to make people happy, but to lead people to abundant living eternally and on earth. This should be a parent's goal as well.

➤ **Like Jesus, parents should be just, strong and respected authority figures.**

Being just, as a parent, means doing what is right for your child. Whatever will benefit a child's spiritual, emotional, intellectual and even physical well being is what a parent should focus on. Making a child happy at whatever cost is not the goal of healthy parenting. A parent's role and goal is to raise well disciplined, respectful and godly children. This can only happen when parents are strong in their convictions and a child respects their authority.

➤ **Having authority is different than being an authoritarian.**

An authoritarian demands obedience using full overpowering control. There is little to no dialogue, instruction and or care for the hearts of those under them. Control and perfection are required at all times. No questions asked or else...

Having parental authority is different from being an authoritarian. Love, rules and boundaries are placed by a good parent in a child's life for the child's well-being.

A parent that exercises their godly role as the authority does so to bring security, joy and health to their child. They are always instructing and are emotionally present. They help their children understand the behavior and character God requires of them.

- **Parents who are permissive for the sake of avoiding conflict will not gain respect and obedience from their children.**

A child will know they can get away with bad behavior if they can play on their parents emotions, and/or lack of persistence and perseverance. Parents should begin adjusting their children's behavior at a very young age. The earlier the training the earlier the compliance and development of healthy well balanced children. A parent's will to raise well-behaved children must be stronger than the will of a child to have authority in the home.

- **Do not justify bad behavior, deal with it. Being wishy washy with a child will only strengthen their carnal nature.**

"The precepts of the Lord are right, giving joy to the heart. The commands of the Lord are radiant, giving light to the eyes." Psalm 19:8

A parent must be consistent and unbending in disciplining their children when unacceptable behavior arises. You must learn what form of discipline is effective for your child.

This may change with age. The Bible clearly teaches that "sparing the rod spoils the child". Trust the Bible over the psychology of culture.

When children are disciplined in their toddler years they are more likely to be well behaved before they are of school age. They have learned to respect their parent's authority and understand there are consequences to disobedience.
Disobedience = Consequence
Obedience = Blessing and Reward

➤ **It is never OK for a child to misbehave and rebel against a parent's authority.**

A child must understand you require proper behavior. Training a child is hard work, but it is a necessary work that will result in having godly children who will accomplish the will of God for their lives.

Use wisdom, intuition and prayer to evaluate why a child may be misbehaving and correct the situation. Sometimes a child is seeking attention, may be learning bad behavior from other children, is not getting proper rest or good nutrition, etc. But even so, do not excuse away bad behavior.

➤ **Make consistent time to talk and pray with your children.**

Bedtime is a good time to pray with and for your children. It is also a good time to communicate and encourage them. If bedtime is at 8PM, begin the process at 7PM. Allow time to pray and talk. But it should never be the only time. Look for special moments to parent your children, like when driving together in a vehicle, going somewhere special, etc. Make time for conversation and bonding to happen. Words such as, I love you, you are so important to me, you are amazing, etc., should always be in your vocabulary. Ask the Holy Spirit to help you.

Interesting
https://dogcare.dailypuppy.com/fun-types-dogs-3772.html

"Alpha dogs are the highest ranking members of packs. They are followed by beta dogs, and then lastly, omega dogs. Alpha dogs possess tough, controlled "take charge" temperaments. They don't follow rules; they dish them out. Beta dogs often have strong temperaments, but are undeniably lower in status than alpha dogs, and therefore accept their positions. Omega dogs, on the other hand, are rather timid and submissive canines. They are not as self-assured as the others, and sometimes are susceptible to being walked all over by the rest."

I am not comparing children to dogs, but it is interesting that every child, like every dog, has a certain temperament. You may have an "Alpha" temperament at home that may require a greater amount of time and diligence than another temperament. The good news is, even Alpha temperaments can be trained to follow instruction and be well behaved.

BOTTOM LINE
- Your child's happiness is not the goal of parenting.
- Having authority is different than being an authoritarian.
- Never justify bad behavior.
- Make consistent time to talk and pray with and for your children.

Small Group Discussion Questions

What really spoke to you in this "Parent Tip"?

What would you change in your parenting because of this "Parent Tip"?

Do you have any suggestions regarding this "Parent Tip" topic?

Today's Prayer

LORD, thank you for giving me the greatest gift in the world, a child. Help me to raise respectful and well behaved children who will honor your commandments. Give me the strength and fortitude to stay strong in my parenting and to not allow the carnal nature to rule in my child's life and in my home. In Jesus' Name, I pray. Amen!

Personal Reflection

Parent Tip #18

REASONING WITH A CHILD

"Honor your father and your mother, so that you may live long in the land the Lord your God is giving you."
Exodus 20:12

The Bible clearly teaches a child to honor his or her mother and father. A child's understanding of the concept of honor increases as they get older and grow into a teenager. A parent cannot expect a toddler or young child to behave properly based upon their ability to reason. A child needs to be taught and told what to do.

> **The younger a child the more the necessity of a parent controlling their behavior.**

Young children should be told what to do as their ability to reason is not yet mature. They must know your laws and commands are to be followed and misbehavior will not be tolerated. Parents must apply the necessary pressure and discipline required to get their children to act properly. This takes work, consistency and a demand for proper behavior.

A child's obstinance and resistance is no reason to give in to improper behavior. Forceful compliance is a necessity when a child is young.

> **You will see some parents trying to reason with their young child(ren) even when their child's behavior is completely out of line.**

The younger a child, the more important it is to set secure boundaries and rules and to control their behavior. A no is a no and that's it! Children must know they cannot disobey without consequence and/or punishment.

You cannot expect your toddler to follow instructions because you said so. You cannot reason with a toddler or younger children. You must have physical boundaries for their protection. Control and discipline is sometimes needed for a child's protection much like a playpen is an appropriate physical protective device. Do not expect young children to have the attention span to sit with you for a teaching lesson or to have the cognitive or emotional ability to understand and obey instruction.

➤ **As children get older their ability to understand and learn increases.**

As a child approaches pre-teen years, a parent can spend more time explaining the whys behind their requirements, rules, boundaries and actions. Parental conversations with your children open up great opportunities for God to speak to them as well. God will use you as a parent to speak into your children's lives, and He will use your children to speak into your life as well.

As long as your child acts like a child, they need to be controlled like a child. As they mature into obedient and respectful children, your parenting can become more focused on teaching, mature discussion and reasoning.

➤ **If a child's bad behavior is controlled when they are younger, they are less likely to rebel against parental control and authority when they enter teenage years.**

The earlier you require obedience by controlling behavior, the less behavior modification a child will need later in life. For sure, strong-willed children take more time and effort than children who are compliant, but the same rules of parenting apply. Diligence, consistency and discipline are necessary in training a child in the way they should go. Do not let a strong-willed child overwhelm you and cause you to back down in requiring obedience. You must work hard at getting every child to respond to you with obedience and respect.

"Train up a child in the way he should go: and when he is old, he will not depart from it." Proverbs 22:6

➤ **If a parent invests in learning how to raise their children with Biblical principles (Parent Tips) and apply them consistently, they will raise honorable children.**

Raising kids by your emotions, convenience, by the example of bad parenting, by the seat of your pants, or by culture's ever-changing methods contrary to the teachings of scripture, will make things harder for you and your children. Pray, learn and work hard on applying the Biblical teachings and principles provided to us by the Lord in scripture in raising children.

Lori's Story

When our children were young, we basically told them what to do. They had a set play time, bath time, bed time, and wake up time. They could only watch certain TV shows and play with certain things and be with certain families. We told them they could not ask for things in front of their friends, such as asking us if a friend could sleep over or vice versa. **If they asked in front of their friend, the answer would automatically be no.**

As our children got older, we would hear them out as they tried to convince mom and dad for certain things. We always thought our son Michael would be a lawyer. He had a way with words, and he was good at debating. At times we would have to have long sit downs with Michael concerning his disagreeing with decisions we had made. He would write long letters and send them down the stairway in the form of a paper airplane. His letters would be filled with scriptural content arguing against our decisions. Michael had come into an age of reasoning with his parents.

We did not see Michael's disagreements as rebellion because he was not being disrespectful. It was important for us and for him to be able to articulate the reasoning for our decisions. This was an opportunity for us to teach versus just tell and require obedience.

Lori's Story (continued)

As children get older it is important to allow them to express their feelings and for them to hear you out as well. I have to say, there were times when Michael was right and got his way. God had used him to show us that sometimes fear was overtaking our parenting. Also, as parents we had to come to a place of trusting God with our children as they became older. We had to trust they would apply the teachings and spirituality they had received at home into their lives as well.

Interesting

The following is taken from -
https://www.scholastic.com/parents/family-life/social-emotional-learning/development-milestones/age-reason.html

Around the age of seven, give or take a year, children enter a developmental phase known as the age of reason. "The age of reason refers to the developmental cognitive, emotional, and moral stage in which children become more capable of rational thought, have internalized a conscience, and have better capacity to control impulses (than in previous stages)," explains *Dana Dorfman*, PhD, psychotherapist, and co-host of the podcast 2 Moms on the Couch.

It's the time when a child starts to truly grasp the difference between right and wrong, and begins to realize that other people have their own feelings that might not match his or hers.

BOTTOM LINE
- The younger a child the more control is a necessity.
- You must tell a young child what to do. Teaching and reasoning is for teen years.
- Early control of behavior will reduce the need for behavior modification later in life.
- Pray, learn and work hard at applying Biblical parenting tips.

Small Group Discussion Questions

What really spoke to you in this "Parent Tip"?

What would you change in your parenting because of this "Parent Tip"?

Do you have any suggestions regarding this "Parent Tip" topic?

Today's Prayer

LORD, I thank you for giving me principles for raising obedient and respectful children. Help me to be diligent in learning how to be a good parent and faithful in applying Biblical parenting in my home. In Jesus' Name, I pray. Amen!

Personal Reflection

(Parent Tip #19)

DIFFERENT STROKES FOR DIFFERENT FOLKS

There was a TV show that ran from 1978 to 1986 called Different Strokes. The sitcom revolved around a white widowed millionaire who adopted two black children. Phil Drummond had promised his housekeeper he would care for her children upon her death. Phil had to learn to parent in a world filled with many challenges, including raising children with racial differences.

> **Every home has challenges.**

In raising 3 children of our own, two boys and one girl, one thing is for sure, every child and family is unique and faces different challenges.

There are homes with a dad and a mom, those with single parents, and homes that have blended families. Raising boys is different from raising girls, and every child is unique. Some children are very active and physical, while others are more subdued. Some children are introverts and others extroverts. Some excel in sports, while others would rather read, draw, play an instrument, etc.

Your challenge as a parent is learning the dynamics of your family and what makes each child tick. Every child is special in their own way and responds to different stimuli and parenting techniques.

➤ **Do all you can to identify your child's unique strengths and gifting.**

God has gifted every person with their own personality, gifts and talents. Thank God Beethoven was put in front of a piano, Michelangelo was given a chisel and a brush, and Steve Jobs had a computer. Give your child opportunities to experiment and find the gifts God has placed inside of them. This helps build self-esteem.

➤ **You cannot raise every child with the same brush stroke. There are different strokes for different folks!**

Biblical principles of parenting should remain steadfast, but application may need to be tweaked for each child. For example, some children are easily guided and disciplined with a strong verbal parental command and or incentives, while others may need a rod of correction. Time out and removal of pleasures are all techniques of discipline. We recommend you never take a child out of a church activity as punishment. This would be counterproductive to their spiritual well being. We also do not believe in sending a child to his or her room as a form of punishment. Isolation and allowing them to seethe in anger and or rebellion is not healthy.

➤ **Obviously child abuse should never be confused with proper discipline.**

The Bible disagrees with the notion that spanking is child abuse. Some parents abuse their children without laying a hand on them.

Our personal opinion is spanking should only be considered after other methods have been exhausted, and only If it works. No one form of discipline works in every case. You have to work at determining what works when and never discipline in anger. Also, take every opportunity to affirm your love for your child after disciplining them and speak encouraging words into their spirit.

> **We understand some people believe spanking should never be an option for discipline.**

There are various reasons for this belief system, including misuse and abuse of spanking, and of course secular teaching against spanking.

For sure a parent should research all forms of behavior modification with the goal of raising obedient and kind hearted children with manners. A child should never be allowed to be lawless.

A Story

Even at a young age children display certain tendencies and likings. My oldest son was drawn to computers and building things, my younger son was always banging on things in rhythm, my daughter was creative and liked to draw. We filled our home with musical instruments, skate ramps, a basketball hoop, a trampoline, bikes, books, action figures, toy guns, swords, dolls, art easels, computers, a video camera for the kids, etc. This provided an opportunity for our children's gifts and talents to be unveiled and to grow. It was also a tool for discipline. We knew what our children did not want taken away from them. We helped direct every one of our children to use their gifts and talents in church, in school, for fun, and for business.

BOTTOM LINE

- Every home and child is different and faces challenges.
- Help identify each child's unique gifts and talents and develop them.
- Biblical principles must remain steadfast in raising children, but application may need tweaking for each child.
- Behavior modification and discipline is a must in raising healthy children.

Small Group Discussion Questions

What really spoke to you in this "Parent Tip"?

What would you change in your parenting because of this "Parent Tip"?

Do you have any suggestions regarding this "Parent Tip" topic?

Today's Prayer

LORD, please give me insight and wisdom as to your purpose for each of my children. Help me to identify their gifts and talents and to develop them to become all they can be. In Jesus' Name, I pray. Amen!

Personal Reflection

Parent Tip #20

MANNERS MATTER

How people behave in society, i.e., at home, at work, in the marketplace, among friends and strangers, says a lot about a person's upbringing and character. You will make a first impression of a person by their manners, how they greet you, respond to you, treat you, and behave in general.

➤ **Manners are important and should be taught at home.**

Without manners human beings become lawless and abased in their actions. Godliness does not exist without self respect, respect for others, kindness, boundaries and consideration of the feelings of others.

Basic manners, such as how to properly acknowledge and address people, how to conduct oneself in various environments, how to eat, speak and act with courtesy, etc. should be taught at a young age.

➤ **Acknowledging people with politeness, with eye contact, and a simple good morning, good evening, hello, handshake, thank you, please, yes sir, no sir, yes ma'am, no ma'am, are basic good manners to teach your children.**

Simple manners can be the difference in how a child and adult advances in society. Manners can be the distinguishing factor that elevates a person in the school classroom, promotes someone in their workplace, and distinguishes the character of Christ in a world filled with disrespect, godlessness and lawlessness.

Manners can also affect a person's ability to have healthy relationships with others.

➤ **Lack of manners will always affect a person's ability to be all God has called them to be.**

Some common manners to teach children should include not picking of the nose in public, not eating with mouth open, not coughing or sneezing without covering, not barging into someone's space without saying excuse me, not eating without washing of hands, not grabbing food over someone at the table, not passing gas in public, and not being rude and addressing people with courtesy.

➤ **Take some time to evaluate manners in your household.**

It's never too late to talk about the importance of manners with your children. Always teach, remind, and model manners. Refining behavior is as important as education and developing skills to become a healthy person and productive member of society.

BOTTOM LINE
- Manners are still important and should be taught at a young age.
- Manners can be the distinguishing factor in advancing in society.
- Manners are a reflection of godliness and the kindness and courtesy of Christ.
- It's never too late to teach manners.

Small Group Discussion Questions

What really spoke to you in this "Parent Tip"?

What would you change in your parenting because of this "Parent Tip"?

Do you have any suggestions regarding this "Parent Tip" topic?

Today's Prayer

LORD, please help me to raise children who have respect for themselves and others and who behave with common courtesy and discipline. May they reflect the character of Christ and exemplify high moral character in all they put their hands to accomplish. In Jesus' Name, I pray. Amen

Personal Reflection

Parent Tip #21

A STRONG WILL CAN BE A FUTURE BENEFIT

Strong-willed children usually need more parental focus, time and attention. You must ask God to help you to discern and identify what causes the heart and mind of every child to be won over. You have to win over your child's will without crushing his or her spirit. This takes time, effort, wisdom and prayer.

No one said parenting was going to be easy, but you will experience the rewards of your labor over time and your children will respect and love you for it.

> **Does each child in your family experience the same attention?**

Do you play favorites because one child is easier to parent than another? It is not unusual to give a compliant child more admiration, affection and affirmation than a strong-willed child. Some parents will even admit they love all their children, but do not always like all their children. Do not feel guilty about your feelings. A child with a strong will can be a handful, but there is a way to have a positive mindset even with a strong-willed child.

Ask God to help you see a strong-willed child as an asset and not a liability. You may have an incredible future leader in your home. If harnessed properly, a strong-willed child can become an amazing godly gift to the world. Ask God for the extra love and patience you need to raise a strong-willed child, and get the wisdom you need to do so.

➤ A child's behavior is influenced by many things.

We all begin with a disadvantage in this world, and that is being born with a carnal, sinful nature. Every human being has a sinful nature, which is bent towards rebellion and sin. The Bible says there is no one that is good, not one! Therefore every child needs to come to Christ and develop a God consciousness. This is one of your most important roles as a parent; developing your child's spirituality and teaching them godliness by example first, then instruction.

Rebellion can come from suppressed feelings, hurt, confusion, physical and/or emotional pain. Take time to know and understand your child. Ask lots of questions and use discernment to determine the cause of their behavior, positive *and* negative. Try to understand the whys behind a child's behavior. Why are they acting out? Why are they sad? Why are they isolating? Why do they not like school? Positive reinforcement, parental consistency and discipline will help bring your child to a place of peace, joy, contentment and obedience.

➤ The highest form of parenting is love.

The highest form of parenting is love, and love is the highest form of spirituality. Never hold back love from your children!

"Whoever does not love does not know God, because God is love." 1 John 4:8

The Bible says God is love. It is impossible to truly define love without God. Love is more than an emotion or a set of words and/or actions. For your children to be whole as spiritual beings, they will need to experience *Agape love* - a love that can only be experienced by a relationship with God. This kind of love touches the deepest part of our being, our spirit being.

Pray constantly for every one of your children and pray with them every day. Bless them when they rise and when they go to bed. Raise them in the House of God and surround them with godly role models and examples. This will take being faithful to God and having an undying spiritual commitment and effort in raising your children.

"Train up a child in the way he should go: and when he is old, he will not depart from it." Proverbs 22:6

➤ Love is deliberate.

Giving of time, affection, undivided attention, making conversation, listening carefully, understanding your child's feelings, making fun and lasting memories, praying with your children, talking about God and issues of importance, having consistent family times, vacation and dinner together (at least 3x per week) etc., all are forms of love. Every child needs and deserves a parent's love. God showed His love by sacrificing His Son Jesus even when we did not deserve or earn it.

Interesting

There was a study published by the US National Library of Medicine https://www.ncbi.nlm.nih.gov/pubmed/26147775 that examined personality traits exhibited by strong-willed children between the ages of 8 and 12 years of age.

They examined 742 children and evaluated them based on things like academic conscientiousness, entitlement and defiance. Forty years later, they were surprised to see a trend. Traits like rule breaking and defiance turned out to be the best non-cognitive predictor of high income as an adult. Again, do not see a strong-willed child as a negative, but rather as an opportunity to mold a future success story.

BOTTOM LINE
- A strong-willed child may have an advantage later in life.
- Take time to know the whys behind your child's behavior, good *and* bad.
- Every child must experience *Agape love* to become a whole person.
- The highest form of parenting is love and love is deliberate.

Small Group Discussion Questions

What really spoke to you in this "Parent Tip"?

What would you change in your parenting because of this "Parent Tip"?

Do you have any suggestions regarding this "Parent Tip" topic?

Today's Prayer

LORD, please help me to raise children who will achieve your purpose for them in life. Help me to navigate my parenting of a strong willed child and to see the great potential in them. Give me the patience, understanding and wisdom to do so. In Jesus' Name, I pray. Amen

Personal Reflection

Parent Tip #22

FREEDOM TO CHOOSE

"Train up a child in the way he should go: and when he is old, he will not depart from it."
Proverbs 22:6

I recently heard a parent say, I am allowing my child to choose their own religion. Allowing a child freedom to choose can be a good thing in their development process, but only if their decisions do not negatively affect their safety, well-being and eternal salvation.

> **God tells us to raise a child in the way they should go.**

We are living in a world that is pressuring parents to allow secular culture to raise their children. Godless, immoral and deceived leaders believe their ways are superior to the tested teachings of scripture.

> **Society is pushing parents to allow children to make their own decisions at any age.**

The reasoning behind giving children the right to make their own decisions at any age is ludicrous and deceptive. Greed, immorality, and demonic influence is pushing this destructive logic and narrative. It is contrary to Biblical teaching and lacks wisdom and common sense.

> **The world says a child should have the right to decide their gender, their sexual preference, when to submit to parents, when to have sex, etc.**

This thinking is based upon the false notion a child has equal rights and has the cognitive ability to make any decision. This mantra is becoming pervasive in the times we are living in.

It opens the door to all kinds of perverted behavior and eliminates parental authority and Biblical moral code. It is lawless, destructive, and disobedient to God and allows the taking advantage of children.

> **A child's thinking, beliefs, and behavior need to be developed and adjusted by parents.**

A parent must be very involved in the lives of their children and will have to battle influences contrary to Biblical teaching. It is the responsibility of a parent to mold a child, not the world.

A parent must raise their children in right environments that foster a Biblical worldview. This takes much thought, investment, parental authority, oversight, and unbending godly leadership. A parent is the only one who has the God-given right to decide what really matters to the physical, emotional and spiritual well-being of their children.

> **Should a child decide if and when to go to church, youth group, school, their religious persuasion or lack of, and other critical decisions?**

The answer is no. As long as a child is under your parental care and support, they should follow the rules of your home. Begin early in training your children in the way they should go, and protect them from worldly indoctrination and godless influences.

➤ **You are your child's protector, and most important influence and advocate.**

Do not let this world take your place as a parent and try to convince you Biblical parenting is outdated and obsolete.

Be the godly parent God empowers and backs you to be!

Interesting

The following information was taken from an article in verywellmind.com written by Kendra Cherry.

https://www.verywellmind.com/what-is-uninvolved-parenting-2794958

Children with uninvolved parents may:
- Be anxious or stressed due to lack of family support
- Be emotionally withdrawn
- Fear becoming dependent on other people
- Have an increased risk of substance abuse
- Have to learn to provide for themselves
- Exhibit more delinquency during adolescence

BOTTOM LINE
- God tells us to raise our children in His ways.
- Society is pushing parents to allow their children to make adult decisions.
- A child should follow the rules of the home.
- A parent is their child's protector and most important influence and advocate.
- Do not let the world become your child's parent.

Small Group Discussion Questions

What really spoke to you in this "Parent Tip"?

What would you change in your parenting because of this "Parent Tip"?

Do you have any suggestions regarding this "Parent Tip" topic?

Today's Prayer

LORD, please help me to protect my children from godless influences. Help me to develop a close relationship with them with open and honest communication. Please keep my children receptive to my guidance and expose anything that would cause them to stray off the path to a blessed life in Christ. In Jesus' Name I pray. Amen

Personal Reflection

(Parent Tip #23)

WHAT DISCIPLINE IS NOT

"If anyone causes one of these little ones—those who believe in me—to stumble, it would be better for them to have a large millstone hung around their neck and to be drowned in the depths of the sea."
Matthew 18:6

It is grieving to hear and see adults losing control with their children. Most of us have seen this type of behavior in public. Hearing any parent, a dad or a mom, berating their children with obscenities, name calling, hurtful gestures and/or physical abuse is never acceptable.

- **It is never Ok for a parent to verbally, emotionally/psychologically or physically abuse a child, no matter what behavior a child is demonstrating.**

Speaking harshly to a child, degrading them, screaming and losing control as an adult, either verbally or physically, is not discipline. We all know parenting can be stressful, and some children really know how to push buttons, but there is no reason to hurt a child emotionally or physically in any way. Control your temper, and wait for an appropriate time to discipline your child - but do not wait long. Even spanking must be done when a parent is in full control and operating in love.

- **Giving up on addressing a child's misbehavior is not acceptable.**

Sometimes the easiest thing to do when a child is misbehaving is to walk away and not address the bad behavior. Yes, as a parent, you should not discipline in anger, but discipline must be forthcoming to bring a child into proper behavior.

If a child knows they can control a parent and get away with bad behavior, they will do so time and time again. The carnal nature of a child will rule.

Even if a child calms down and changes their behavior, not addressing bad behavior teaches disrespect towards authority.

For example, if a child refuses to eat what is provided to them, the easiest thing to do is to give them what they want, even if it is not a healthy choice. The better decision would be to take the food away and set it aside for a later time. The child must be required to eat what you as a parent provide to them. When they get hungry enough they will eat.

▶ **Isolation is not a good discipline technique.**

Putting a child in their room when they are rebelling against a parent is not a good idea. It is not healthy emotionally and spiritually to send a child to their room when they are angry and their emotions are high. A spirit of hatred, bitterness, anger, rebellion, unforgiveness, etc. will speak to them in their isolation. It is better to deal with things as they happen and out in the open. You do not want your child ingesting lies into their minds and fuming while alone in their room.

▶ **Be careful to not allow your child to manipulate you.**

It is amazing to see how intelligent and manipulating a child can be. If a child knows a certain behavior will cause their parents to give in to their desires, they will exercise that behavior, both good and bad.

Do not let your child manipulate you. This will cause disrespect towards authority. If there are other children in the house observing the manipulation, they will disrespect you as well. Allowing a child to manipulate you will only hurt the godly relational order you should have with your children, and it can become a habit pattern.

> **Fostering peace by not disciplining a child is not peace.**

Peace is not peace if there is rebellion against a parent in the home. You may get your child to calm down by giving them what they want, but this is not true peace. That is a temporary truce.

Discipline is how a parent brings their children into becoming healthy, stable and secure people. When there is proper discipline in the home, true harmony can exist.
You do not want to create a little tyrant or dictator that has learned how to run the house through manipulation and or rebellion. Fostering peace by not disciplining a child is not peace. This never fixes the underlying issue of misbehavior.

"No discipline seems pleasant at the time, but painful. Later on, however, it produces a harvest of righteousness and peace for those who have been trained by it." Hebrews 12:11

➤ Figure out what form of discipline works for your child.

Do all you can to muster up the energy, stick-to-itiveness, and spirituality, to be the parent you are called to be. True peace comes only when a home has a godly and Biblical order to it and it is filled with the fruit of the Spirit.

"But the fruit of the Spirit is love, joy, peace, forbearance, kindness, goodness, faithfulness, gentleness and self-control." Galatians 5:22-23

A Story

As pastors who work with families daily, we sometimes hear parents of challenging children say "I just can't take it anymore." These are real emotions being experienced by good people. It is not easy living in a world that demands so much from parents, i.e., work, school, bills, etc. The problem is we cannot give up, we have children who are counting on us. We have to find strength through God, prayer, a church community, family, friends and whatever other support is available to us.

At our church, Legacy Church RI, we often use the tag line, "Don't Do Life Alone." Parents need other parents for support, and children need other children to model good behavior to them.

We have seen many parents get the support and help they need through spirituality, good local church communities, and following the "Parent Tips" being provided.

We all have times when we get overwhelmed, but there is comfort and strength through prayer, worship, the presence and empowerment of the Holy Spirit and good friendships.

BOTTOM LINE
- It is never Ok for a parent to verbally or physically abuse a child.
- Giving up on addressing a child's misbehavior is not acceptable.
- Isolation is not a good discipline technique.
- Fostering peace by not disciplining a child is not peace.
- Figure out what form of discipline works for your child.
- Find support when you get weary as a parent.

Small Group Discussion Questions

What really spoke to you in this "Parent Tip"?

What would you change in your parenting because of this "Parent Tip"?

Do you have any suggestions regarding this "Parent Tip" topic?

Today's Prayer

LORD, please help me to be a strong Spirit-filled parent. Give me the energy, discernment and wisdom in determining how to address and adjust my children's behavior patterns. Help me to find the support needed when I get weary and fill me with the power of your Holy Spirit. Bless my home with your favor and peace. In Jesus' Name I pray. Amen

Personal Reflection

(Parent Tip #24)

YOUR CHILD HAS A DESTINY

"Many are the plans in a person's heart, but it is the LORD's purpose that prevails." Proverbs 19:21

A good parent always has aspirations for their children. Moms and dads want to see every child do well in school, excel in their careers, have successful jobs and thrive in their personal relationships. It is honorable for a parent to help their children to excel in life.

- **Matching the desires of a parent to the purposes of God for their child(ren) should always be a goal.**

Pray and ask the LORD to guide you in identifying your child's natural gifts and talents. You must remember every child belongs to God. It is He who created them, gifted them and has a specific purpose for them.

"Before I formed you in the womb I knew you, before you were born I set you apart; I appointed you as a prophet to the nations." Jeremiah 1:5

Can you imagine if a famous composer like Beethoven was not put in front of a piano or an artist like Michelangelo was not given a brush for painting or a chisel for sculpting? Expose your children to as many things as possible to draw out of them the gifts placed in them by God.

> **King David's father saw him as a shepherd boy. God saw Him as a King.**

In the Bible, the First Book of Samuel and the First Book of Chronicles both identify David as the son of Jesse, the Bethlehemite, and as the youngest of eight sons. Jesse needed David to help with the family estate and to protect his livestock from being ravaged by wild animals. Someone in the family had to tend to their food and income source. Jesse chose David.

Even when the Prophet Samuel came to the home of Jesse to seek the next king of Israel, Jesse did not consider David. He did not see his youngest son as a worthy candidate. The plans of God for David did not match up to the plans of his father for him. David was chosen by his father for a lowly position of caring for a flock of sheep. God had higher plans. Do all you can as a parent to seek the higher plans of God for the life of your child. Just keep everything within the context of Biblical living and morals.

> **Do not underestimate the purpose of God for your child.**

Even at an early age, a parent should do all they can to identify the gifts given by God to their child. Does your child have great motor skills, musical abilities, excellent reading and comprehension, great communication skills, do other children tend to follow your child's lead? Does your child have a profound interest in building things, organizing, spirituality, helping people, etc.?

Try to further develop whatever you see your child drawn to, and areas of aptitude in which they excel. If it's music, have them try different instruments. If it's building things, get them toys that challenge them in this area. If it's reading, get them great books. If it's public speaking, have them listen to the greatest preachers and orators in history, etc.

➤ **You will often see children following their parent's footsteps, good *and* bad.**

What you do not want to do as a parent is force your child to become what you desire for them versus what God may have planned for them. It is better to pray for the purpose of God for your child's life and to identify and develop the gifts God has placed in them.

Teachers, family members, church leaders, and others who spend time with your children, will sometimes be those who identify your child's giftings and talents. Ask others what they see in your child. You will be amazed at what they may see and say.

"Plans fail for lack of counsel, but with many advisers they succeed." Proverbs 15:22

➤ **Not every child is born to be a doctor. Every child has a different IQ, aptitude and skills.**

Do not compare your child to others. Every child is unique. It is ok if your child does not attend college, but rather pursues a trade or something that truly interests them. For sure you have to encourage and train your child to do their best at everything set before them and to not be lazy. You do not want your child on their cell phone rather than completing homework. At the same time, you do not want to put extreme demands on a child for the sake of family pride, parental ego, living your personal aspirations through them, or to appease culture.

➤ **There must be a healthy balance in fostering the growth of a healthy well-adjusted child.**

You do not want to raise a child driven by fear, an extreme desire for approval, and extremely overwhelmed by the pressure to succeed. At the same time, you do not want to raise a child who cannot handle the challenges of life, or a child that is lazy.

"Lazy hands make for poverty, but diligent hands bring wealth."
Proverbs 10:4

Interesting

In 2013, Pew Research conducted a survey that said 64% of parents believe not enough pressure is put on children to do well in school. This may be true. As a parent, you must use wisdom in directing your child's attention and focus. Assess your motivations for your children, and pray for direction. Be careful to not be overly demanding, but do incentivize and encourage your children to work hard and have achievements in their lives.

A Story

My wife and I have pastored many people and have seen different styles of parenting. Some people are authoritarian in nature, while others are more laid back. Whatever a parent's personality, it does not really matter in parenting. The principles of parenting remain the same. You want to raise children with the greatest amount of love, faith, guidance, direction, and wisdom to succeed in what God has designed and called them to be and do. You may not know the ultimate purpose of God for your child, but you can prepare them to be successful, open to the will of God and to be happy.

We have seen some parents exercise unrealistic expectations, pressure and demands on their children. Demanding perfection in every area of life and making routine so stringent as to take away the wonder, freedom and happiness of just being a child is not healthy.

A Story (continued)

I remember a family raising their children in an extremely structured home with the highest of expectations and demands. It reminded me of the Von Trapp family as portrayed in the movie *The Sound of Music*. The children were being raised in a militaristic home environment until the new governess, played by actress Julie Andrews, brought a healthy dose of childhood play back into the household.

The children of this family excelled in school and spoke multiple languages. They were well-behaved, but it was very rare to see a smile on their faces. The joy of just being a child was not evident in their lives. You do not want to raise robots that perform tasks but have no human emotion and joy in their lives. You want to raise well-balanced children with lots of room to have fun, while achieving all God has for them in this world.

BOTTOM LINE

- Pray for the plans of God to come to fruition in the life of your child.
- Identify gifts and talents early on and groom them.
- Do not compare your child with others, your child is unique.
- Allow your child to experience childhood without undue pressure and demands.
- You want your child to succeed, but not strong-armed to meet unrealistic expectations.

Small Group Discussion Questions

What really spoke to you in this "Parent Tip"?

What would you change in your parenting because of this "Parent Tip"?

Do you have any suggestions regarding this "Parent Tip" topic?

Today's Prayer

LORD, please help me to raise happy well-adjusted children who achieve your will in their lives. Show me the talents and giftings of my children and how to enhance their progress in being all you are calling them to be. In Jesus' Name I pray, Amen

Personal Reflection

Parent Tip #25

BRING ON THE LAUGHTER

"A cheerful heart is good medicine, but a crushed spirit dries up the bones." Proverbs 17:22

Can something as simple as laughter benefit our families, marriages, parental relationships, and even promote spiritual, emotional and physical health? The answer is yes. Many studies are proving what the Bible has been saying for thousands of years, *"A cheerful heart is good medicine."*

➤ **Laughter is necessary and beneficial to our health, just like food and water.**

This life lasts for only a few short years, and taking things too seriously without adding laughter and enjoyment into our lives is not only unhealthy, but unbearable.

An article written by the Mayo Clinic Staff brings much illumination to the importance of laughter. In addition to increasing endorphins in the brain, which makes you feel happier, laughter enhances the intake of oxygen and stimulates organs and physical functions, such as your heart, lungs and muscles.

(https://www.mayoclinic.org/healthy-lifestyle/stress-management/in-depth/stress-relief/art-20044456)

Laughter has a unique way of soothing tension and reducing stress by improving circulation and relaxing muscles. It improves your overall immunity system as it combats negative feelings and stress that create harmful chemicals in the body. The less stress, the better your feelings and mood.

The better your mood, the better your relationships with people around you, including your children. Thus, laughter can help you be a better and more likable parent.

Some studies found mood also affects your immune system and brings about illness. WebMD reports that a doctor by the name of Lee Berk, MD, a University of California Irvine medical professor, along with his associates, have found a person's mood serves a role in fighting viruses, bacteria, cancer and heart disease. *"Laughter is good medicine"* just as the Bible says.

Is laughter necessary to your health? Absolutely! But just as important, laughter benefits your spiritual and emotional health, and having healthy, happy relationships with your children and others.

➤ **Be intentional about bringing more laughter into your life and home.**

There are some people that make you laugh. Get around them. Or maybe you are the type of person that loves making others laugh. What a gift! Use it!

Plan having fun times just for a laugh. Have a family movie night and watch a hysterical movie. Play some fun games that make people laugh. I know every time we play the game of Spoons, we experience belly laughs.

During daytime hours, take a break, get lighthearted and find something amusing to laugh about. Do all you can to laugh every day!

A Story

There are some things that happen at home that are better off left unsaid. For the sake of this writing I will share. There are moments when this dad breaks out into a funny dance. I try my best to do some Michael Jackson spins, leg movements, slides, popping, etc. The result is family laughter and my kids pulling out their phones to record these momentous moments. Joking around makes for family bonding and fun memories that will carry on long after I am gone.

Family times filled with laughter are some of the most memorable moments of our lives. Reminiscing about stupid things done and funny things that happen bring great joy to the home. We need more time, not less, when we put all seriousness aside and just enjoy each other and laugh. Laughter is the best free medicine one can take!

Interesting

In the British Psychological Society's journal, an article published by Marc Hye-Knudsen, a humor researcher and lab manager, discusses how humor can benefit kids. He found that embarrassing children a little can help them grow into healthy adults. He does not mean being hurtful, but being silly with them in front of friends. Things like dad jokes can help teach kids how to handle awkward moments and the importance of being light hearted.

BOTTOM LINE
- The Bible teaches laughter is good medicine.
- Laughter is spiritually, emotionally and physically beneficial.
- Be intentional about bringing laughter into your home and relationships.
- Laughing more can help you be a better and more likable person and parent.

Small Group Discussion Questions

What really spoke to you in this "Parent Tip"?

What would you change in your parenting because of this "Parent Tip"?

Do you have any suggestions regarding this "Parent Tip" topic?

Today's Prayer

LORD, please help me to give my cares over to you and become more childlike in not having to carry the burdens of the world. Help me to see the benefit of lightheartedness and laughter and to find ways of bringing laughter into my life and home. Help me to not take myself too seriously and to develop the playful part of me. In Jesus' Name I pray. Amen

Personal Reflection

Parent Tip #26

PRAY, PRAY, PRAY

"Do not be anxious about anything, but in everything by prayer and supplication with thanksgiving let your requests be made known to God." Philippians 4:6

There are times in life when there is nothing else to do but pray. When things do not go as expected or work as anticipated, we can still find great hope and solace through prayer. Prayer should not be the action of last resort, but rather a normal part of our daily lives.

Bring prayer into your home and into your child(ren)'s routine.

➤ Pray Before School

One of the greatest lessons you can teach your children is they are not alone. They can ask God to be with them throughout the day. Prayer is a great way to start each day with your children. Teach them by example how to pray. Be deliberate about having them pray.

You will be amazed at the spirituality of children. The inner spirit of a child is created to have a relationship with God our Father. Prayer develops this relationship and makes it personal. It also creates a deeper relationship between a child and his or her parent(s). Prayer binds families together. It is often said, *families that pray together stay together.*

▶ Pray Before Bed

One of the greatest ways to develop closeness with your child is to spend time talking, reading, sharing scripture, telling stories and praying with them. You can make bed time very special by spending quality time with your children.

Establish a routine to talk and listen to your children, their fears, concerns, joys, questions, and always end the night with prayer. Pray for whatever your child desires. It is amazing how perceptive children are to others' needs, as well as their own.

▶ Pray For Personal Needs, For Each Other and For Others

"And I will do whatever you ask in my name, so that the Father may be glorified in the Son." John 14:12

God wants to show your children He hears prayer and He will accomplish His will in our lives. The Bible teaches us to bring our requests before the Lord. Making a prayer list with your children may be a great way to make prayer a priority. Check off prayers answered and take time to talk about trusting in God's goodness and will.

Praying for others is a great way to expand your child's compassion and mindset. The world is much bigger than our own needs. Help your child care for the needs of others by praying for them.

There will be prayers that may not be answered as expected. This provides you as a parent the opportunity to develop your child's faith and knowledge of God's will, timing and His Word.

➤ The Lord's Prayer

Jesus gave us a model for prayer, which we call *"The Lord's Prayer."* This is one prayer worthy of memorization.

*"**After this manner therefore pray ye:** Our Father which art in heaven, Hallowed be thy name. Thy kingdom come, Thy will be done on earth, as it is in heaven. Give us this day our daily bread. And forgive us our debts, as we forgive our debtors. And lead us not into temptation, but deliver us from evil: For thine is the kingdom, and the power, and the glory, forever. Amen."*
Matthew 6:9-13

There are important elements to this prayer, including honoring God, praying for His will, praying for earthly needs, repentance from sin, forgiveness for others, protection from temptation, and declaration of His sovereignty over our lives. Think about such things as you pray and teach your children to pray.

A Story

The daily routine at our home, included prayer and reading. Of course as dad, rough housing was part of our nightly vigil with our two first born children (boys, of course). My wife preferred a calmer end of the day, but *boys will be boys*.

Praying with our children often ended up in great conversations about God. Kids have a way of asking interesting questions, such as **"why did God make skin?"** Often one of our children would answer the question. In this case, the answer was **"to hold your bones in!"** Prayer ends up in laughter, enjoying each other and learning more about our God, a loving, kind, compassionate and fun God!

Interesting

Indian J Psychiatry. 2009 Oct-Dec; 51(4): 247–253.
https://www.ncbi.nlm.nih.gov/pmc/articles/PMC2802370/

There are many articles regarding studies done on the effect of prayer. This one article, highlighted above, was published by the Indian Journal of Psychiatry, and is found in the National Library of Medicine. As Christians we understand it is faith that pleases God, but many scientific studies do show prayer impacts our natural world. As the Bible says, *faith can move mountains!*

"...Truly I tell you, if you have faith as small as a mustard seed, you can say to this mountain, 'Move from here to there,' and it will move. Nothing will be impossible for you." Matthew 17:20

BOTTOM LINE

- Bring prayer into your child(ren)'s routine.
- Pray before school.
- Pray at bedtime.
- Pray for needs, for each other, and for others.
- Pray the Lord's Prayer and learn from it as a model of prayer.

Small Group Discussion Questions

What really spoke to you in this "Parent Tip"?

What would you change in your parenting because of this "Parent Tip"?

Do you have any suggestions regarding this "Parent Tip" topic?

Today's Prayer

LORD, please help me to make prayer a normal part of our daily lives. Help me to raise up children that know how to pray and that see God as a good and loving Father who cares for every need. In Jesus' Name, I pray! Amen!

Personal Reflection

PRAISE FOR PARENT TIPS

"In this ever-changing world full of many challenges, Parent Tips by Ron & Lori Termale is a book of wisdom designed to help you accomplish the universal goal shared by all parents— to raise children to become spiritually and mentally stable, honest, compassionate, contributing members of society. Ron & Lori have successfully done so and any parent can glean from their wisdom."

- ***Cherie Adams***, *multi-award winning recording artist and author of* **MEET MOYD**

"Parenting Tips is an eye opening teaching tool that is easy to follow, and is full of concise lessons on one of the most, if not the most, important job in life….parenting. Ron & Lori Termale have themselves, learned & utilized these Parenting Tips over the years, and have ministered & encouraged countless families to implement them.

Parenting is like 'building the boat in the water'. It is 'on the job training'. These tips prepare you for what you 'shall' face, and provide input for what you're 'currently' facing, in rearing your child. Having a clue instead of being 'clueless' of navigating parenting life is vital. Parents, Mom, Dad, childcare workers ….you will receive common sense & God sense in these pages, to skill you well, in the parenting journey!

This is a much needed resource for parents to guide & guard the formative years of their child. The reader will benefit if they want to develop parental 'convictions' based on principles & practicals found in this book. Parenting is the job of a lifetime!! This will help you!"

- ***Stephen & Nancy Boyce***, *Founding Pastors of New Life/Awakening Church & New Life Leadership Ministries*

"**Parent Tips** is an absolute must-have for any parent seeking practical, and actionable advice in the often-challenging world of raising children. Each of the twenty-six individual tips that Ron and Lori Termale have addressed let me know they understand the real-life struggles parents face, offering down-to-earth strategies that are easy to implement, regardless of where you are on your parenting journey.

What really sets this book apart is its balance of warmth, wisdom, and real-world practicality. The tips aren't just theoretical – they are rooted in everyday situations that every parent will recognize, making each one incredibly relatable. Whether you're a new parent, or just now navigating toddler tantrums, or help your teen through tough decisions, you will find clear, concise guidance that gives you confidence as a parent.

Whether you use this book as a resource for the moment, or a devotional to enlarge you parental vision, you will gain valuable insight and peace of mind, knowing you are on the right path when it comes to raising your children. **Parent Tips** receives my full-throated endorsement!"

- ***Dr. Jerry W David***, *Author and Lecturer, Commonsense Parenting, Raising Principled Children in an Ever-Shifting Culture*

"It is refreshing to read a book that you know is a true testament to the author's way of life. I had the privilege of being the teachers of Ron and Lori's children in their high school years. And I can say that they truly embody the principles laid out by their parents in this book. Today, all their adult children love Jesus, the Church and they are fulfilling their calling in life. This book displays the principles and life applications that have blessed their own children and can bless yours as well."

- ***Marco and Lindsay DeBarros***, *Lead Pastors, New Life South Coast*

"This book is a gift to the body of Christ. Ron and Lori Termale bring wisdom, experience and a legacy of children and grandchildren who love the Lord and passionately follow Jesus. We've personally benefited from conversations with them about raising children so I'm grateful that they've produced this faithful book so that more parents can be resourced and encouraged in parenting just as we have been."

*- **David De La Cruz**, Pastor, Awakening Church and*
***Jessica De La Cruz**, State Senator and Minority Leader*

"Chock-full of practical, biblical and refreshing tips for parents in today's seemingly confusing world of 'anything goes' child-rearing practices. As a Montessori educator and administrator for nearly 30 years, I have seen first hand the unnecessary struggles parents bring upon themselves as they surrender their authority to their children. One of the biggest takeaways from this book is the child's desire for order and discipline. Active parental involvement, established routines and biblical instruction, in a home filled with love and laughter, serve to nurture the whole child.

The self-reflection opportunities throughout Parent Tips are great for encouraging parents to reflect on their own hearts and parenting practices. There is no perfect parent, but there is simple wisdom and discernment to be gained through relationship with God, lots of prayer, and seeking the wise counsel of people like Ron and Lori."

*- **Brenda Medeiros**, Montessori Educator & Administrator*

"As a parent, teacher, former Foster mom, Mentor, Sunday School teacher and presently, a Director in an Early Childhood School, I find this book of "Parent tips" to be not only phenomenal for parents, but an essential Life Guide in relationships. Although there are other Parenting books out there, this particular one is unprecedented in its authenticity of real experiences. It is filled with wisdom nuggets! Designed and organized so well for easy retention, along with the prayers so thoughtfully written. This is a must have in your home's library to be used as a reference guide and a devotional for the family. You will get so much out of it right from the Acknowledgements, Introduction and all the way through to Parent Tip #26."

- ***Gina Murray***, *Program Director of Buttonwoods School for Young Children*

"This book is an invaluable resource for everyone: new parents, parents of older children, and even couples who are preparing to embark on the journey of parenthood. It addresses a wide array of topics that, in today's society, have often become difficult or uncomfortable to discuss. Yet, with the clarity of Biblical wisdom and a deep sense of grace, Pastors Ron and Lori Termale offer practical guidance on how to correct habits that may need transformation within the family. Their words are filled with such profound love and the power of the Holy Spirit, touching the heart and soul of every reader. We've had the privilege of knowing Pastor Ron and Lori since we were in our 20s, and their passion for serving others and their dedication to following God's calling has always been a source of inspiration to us. Their wisdom has grown through the years, and this book is a beautiful reflection of their experience, love, and unwavering commitment to helping families thrive in their walk with Christ. What makes this book so powerful is that it's not just a one-time read. It serves as a daily source of wisdom and reflection, offering practical applications and reminders that help us align our homes with God's perfect design. Every chapter invites us to reconsider our priorities, to cultivate a home grounded in faith, and to raise children with purpose and divine guidance. I am especially grateful for the boldness of the Termales as parents and spiritual leaders. Their willingness to address these critical family issues with courage and compassion is truly inspiring. This is a book that will undoubtedly leave a lasting impact on anyone who reads it."

- ***Alessandro and Isabelle Russo***, Pastors, Vive Church, Rome, Italy

"Pastor Ron and Lori Termale have produced a must-have resource for any parent, children's church worker, or teacher. The practical wisdom and insights they share are grounded in real-life experience as pastors and parents who have raised three children, now adults with families of their own. Each chapter is filled with meaningful advice, personal stories, and relevant Scripture, offering a roadmap for raising children with intention and faith. As Psalm 127:3 says, 'Don't you see that children are God's best gift? The fruit of the womb, His generous legacy?' Ron and Lori not only understand this truth, but they live it, making this book an invaluable guide for anyone committed to raising children with love, faith, and purpose. **Highly recommended!**"

- ***Mike Servello, Sr. and Barb Servello***, *founding pastors Redeemer Church, and non-profit Compassion Coalition.*

"*Parenting Tips* is a practical and easy-to-read book for any parent in today's modern world! Pastor Ron and Lori share their wisdom and insights, equipping parents with the essential tools to raise their children effectively. As a Mom of three boys, I am grateful to apply these tips into my own parenting journey!"

- ***Eva M. Termale***, *Bachelor of Arts in Psychology and Mom to three crazy boys*

"Parents, if you want to raise healthy children in these turbulent times, this book is a must-read! It's packed with practical, easy to implement strategies that will help you grow while building strong resilient kids. The battle for the future of our nation starts in the home. Ron and Lori have given you a blueprint that works! We can say that with confidence because our children grew up with their children and are living proof that these ideas work! Don't just parent—lead your children into their God-given destiny!"

- ***Lance Wallnau***, *Author, CEO, Lance Learning Group & Lance Wallnau Show and Annabelle Wallnau, Founder, Furnishing Families of Texas*

ABOUT THE AUTHORS

Ron and Lori currently lead Legacy Church in Rhode Island as Pastors. Ron also serves on the Board of Directors for Awakening Church in Rhode Island and New Life Southcoast in New Bedford, MA. In the past, the couple helped establish a local daycare and an accredited high school, where Ron briefly served as principal.

Ron holds a Bachelor of Science degree from Bryant University and an MBA from Providence College. Before transitioning to full-time ministry, he worked as a Commercial Bank Vice President. Lori holds an associate's degree from the Community College of Rhode Island.

Above all, Ron and Lori's greatest passion is their love for God and their family. Over the years, they have dedicated themselves to counseling, teaching, and supporting hundreds of families, continuing their mission to foster strong parents, marriages and families.

Email: **LegacyChurchRI@gmail.com** for speaking engagements

FAMILY
LIFE

Ron and Lori Termale are proud parents of three grown children and grandparents to six. Their eldest son, Michael, lives in Nashville with his wife, Britney, and their three children. Michael works as a Producer and Senior Editor for the *Trinity Broadcasting Network (TBN)*. Their middle son, Daniel, is a Senior Growth Marketing Manager at a startup specializing in Artificial Intelligence (AI). Carissa, the youngest, is an entrepreneur and the owner of *Sol Coffee Cart*, a mobile coffee business. She also enjoys working with children and serves as a nanny. All three children, along with their spouses, Britney and Eva, hold leadership positions at various churches.

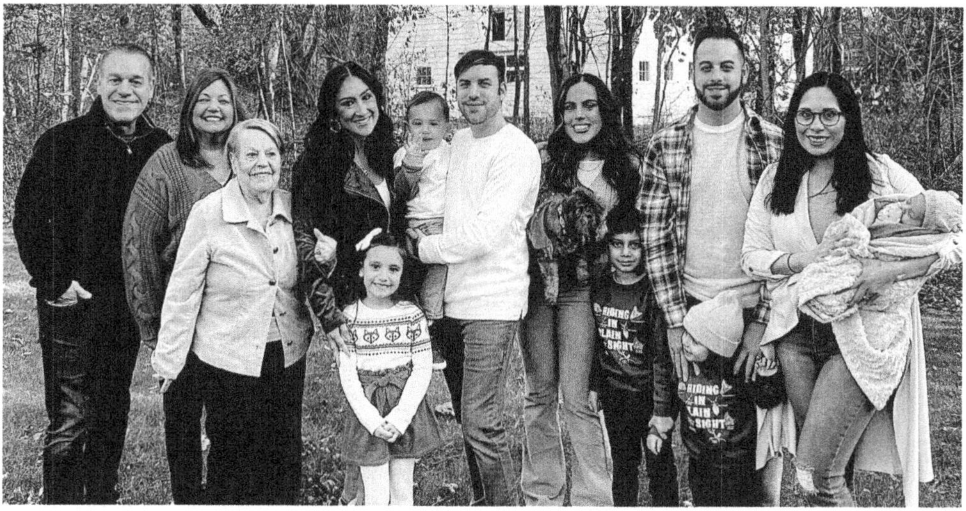

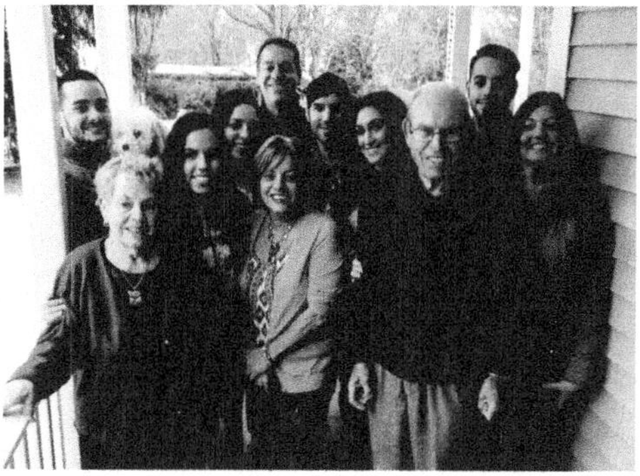

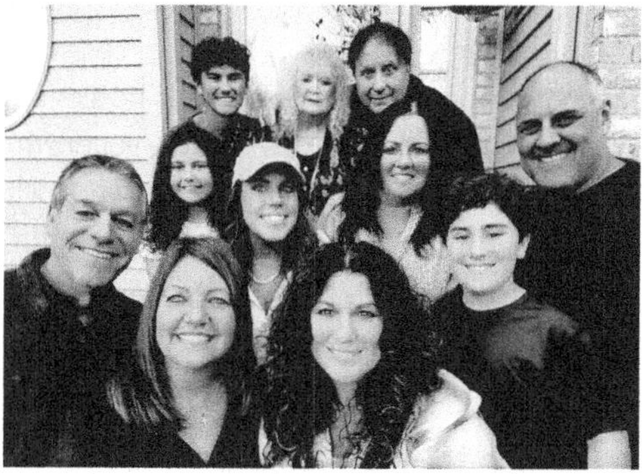

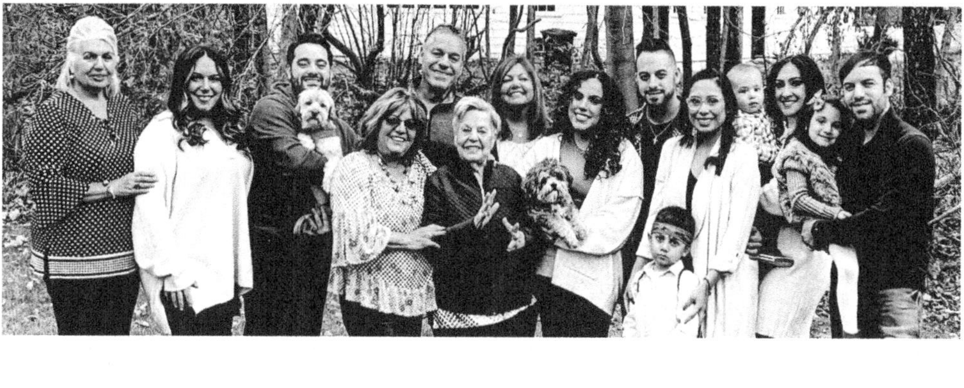

ABOUT OUR PARENTS

"I have had the incredible privilege of growing up with Pastors Ron and Lori as my parents. My parents have always been sold out to Christ, building his church and serving others. They have walked the walk throughout my entire life as genuine ambassadors of Christ, servant leaders, disciples, good stewards, pastors, teachers, and prayer warriors.

I've had to stop and ponder many times over the years of how many thousands of lives they have touched after closing in on nearly 40 years in the ministry. Their integrity and passion to reach people and advance the Gospel has left an indelible mark on us, their children. Because of their example, and the principles that they instilled in us since childhood, their 3 children have lived incredibly blessed lives.

Each parent tip in this book is not only derived from our families lived experiences, but through the hundreds if not thousands of families we have rubbed shoulders with through decades of building a local church, counseling many parents, and gleaning from many pastors and leaders.

If there is one takeaway from this book - it is that these Biblically based principles work. Principles don't change with new generations. These are foundational morals and God inspired ideas and structure that work when applied to any single family - no matter what that family looks like. While children's personalities can vary, God's value system and instructions apply to all of us. Principles are the bedrock and true north that will keep the family unit together, strong, and healthy."

- Michael Termale

"As I grew up, a middle child, I watched my parents pour their hearts into serving God and caring for others. Their dedication was a living example of faith in action. I learned early on that having Christian or pastor parents didn't automatically mean I'd choose the same path; I saw families where ministry overshadowed being present at home, leading to an unhealthy balance. But for my siblings and me, it was different. We didn't just hear our parents' words; we witnessed their sacrifices and the love that filled our home. Those moments inspired us to embrace the same values, igniting a desire to create loving, nurturing families of our own."

- Dan Termale

ABOUT OUR PARENTS

"I am incredibly grateful for the childhood my parents created for me. Whether it was creating songs, going on fun filled vacations, eating around the dinner table every night or having a family game night, every moment was intentional & made for the most memorable childhood. The way my parents deeply love people & genuinely invest into other's lives has been the greatest example to me. They practice what they preach in every aspect of life. Their unwavering support, encouragement & example has shaped me into who I am today. I couldn't be more proud to have them as my parents and I hope to be just like them as parents to my future children."
- *Carissa Termale*

"I have been honored to know Ron & Lori Termale for over 17 years. In that time, I have seen them lead with an anointing so pure and authentic. Not only have they transformed and blessed many families through their ministry but they did it all while raising an upstanding family of their own. Too often we see families fall apart. I am blessed to be married to their son, Michael, and to see first hand how this family has grown together through the years. The biggest testament to their ministry is their children. Each one serving in ministry and living a life that honors God. I pray this book shares some of the incredible wisdom I have gained from observing their leadership through the years. I know these principles will help you navigate even the toughest seasons of parenting."
- *Britney Termale,* Daughter-in-law

"My in-laws are truly remarkable people. From the moment I first met them, they made me feel welcomed, loved and valued. Not only have I witnessed firsthand their faithfulness, loyalty and commitment to serving and building God's House, but I've seen them equally prioritize our family; instilling their faith and being great role models for their children and now grandchildren. I am overwhelmed with gratitude in knowing my three sons have the best Papa and Nonna! From marital advice and parenting tips to the best Italian meals, I feel blessed to be a part of the legacy they're building."
- *Eva M. Termale,* Daughter-in-law

NOTES

NOTES

NOTES

NOTES

Made in United States
North Haven, CT
08 February 2025